Raising A Dragon

The Art of Parenting
The Child with Asperger's
With a Sense of Humor

Debra Townsend

ILLUSTRATIONS BY THE AUTHOR AND BRENDAN TOWNSEND

Raising A Dragon

The Art of Parenting
The Child with Asperger's
With a Sense of Humor

Copyright 2012 Debra Townsend

Published by
Dunes Publishing
Thompsonville, MI 49683

ISBN: 978-0-9852442-0-0
All Rights Reserved

For more information please contact
dunespublishing@gmail.com

"Me"   1-23-97

Acknowledgements

Brendan Townsend

Mark Borchelt

Nicola Conraths-Lange

Brittany Townsend

Monique Townsend

Anne-Marie Oomen

Roger & Sheila Christensen

Caroline Zeigler

Wendy Masterson

Thomas & Kari Townsend

Valeria Thomas

Jed Jaworski

John Pahl

Sharon Randolph

Victoria Lunato

Alex David

Bridgit & Keith Frank

Norm Bistodeau

Steve Cox

Joel Howe

Heath Green

Sander Weckstein

Melanie Kreider

Contents

Contents

Prologue

The idea behind this book is to help parents of children diagnosed with Asperger's Syndrome to better understand them, in hopes of turning parenting these eccentric children into a welcomed and cherished experience.

The insights offered through the eyes of my son Brendan, an amazing young man with AS, have taught me to hear more clearly the language spoken by these unique individuals, who see things from a different perspective. I have learned during our years together, more is often gained by listening to the rhythms of their different drums, than by attempting to teach them to match the cadence of the rest of the band.

In this book I have recounted a few amusing moments from my son's adventure to adulthood, demonstrating many of the main characteristics exhibited by those with Asperger's Syndrome. It is my hope that other parents of AS children might see similarities in their own experiences, and draw upon these humorous stories (along with the AS characteristics they illustrate) to help them to take what can often be frustrating as a parent, and turn it into a remarkably fun and rewarding journey.

When a counselor suggested my son might have Asperger's Syndrome, I had never heard the term, and wondered what it meant. As a side note, Asperger's is correctly pronounced with a hard "g", as in the word good.

Asperger's Syndrome is defined as a category of high-functioning autism, though the definition keeps evolving as more and more children are diagnosed. In general, those with AS have a significantly high intelligence level, and fewer difficulties with speech than classic autism, although many of the same behaviors are exhibited.

The name, Asperger's Syndrome, originates from work done by Hans Asperger, a Viennese pediatrician who published a doctoral thesis regarding the condition in 1944, describing a study group of 4 unusual boys who were similar to each other. Asperger noted the condition usually affected boys, and they were very unusual in how they dealt with social issues, friendships, and conversations. They also exhibited little empathy, moved differently, and each had an absorbing focus of interest.

Asperger originally called this condition, "autistic psychopathy". Although there are overlapping areas of symptoms with classic autism, the differences are also quite apparent. A later paper published by Lorna Wing actually titled the condition using Asperger's name in 1981, due to his extensive research on the subject prior to her own dissertation.

The paper written by Lorna Wing helps set the criteria for Asperger's diagnosis, and asserts the most prevalent characteristic is their difficulty with relating to others in social situations.

This lack of social intelligence typically contributes to years of awkwardness in fitting into mainstream society. Like the sense of inferiority felt by the young swan in the childhood story, *The Ugly Duckling*, this can be devastating to a child. With the importance given to conformity in today's society, this requires special consideration to support a healthy self-esteem during the child's growth.

The responsibility for fostering a healthy self-image, and instilling pride in the potential benefits of their differences, often falls to the parents of an AS child. In my experience, few adults are ready for this challenge as young parents. Having been taught conformity as members of the baby-boomer generation; we are often left in a place where our own viewpoints are the first thing that must be adjusted. In order to accept and embrace these children for who they are, we must first see their uniqueness as exceptional.

Admittedly, my initial reaction to Brendan being diagnosed with Asperger's Syndrome was panic. *My child has a type of autism?* The diagnosis threw me into parental shock, leaving me feeling as though I had counted his toes wrong at birth. Fears of life-altering difficulties that would limit my child and our family forever began to strangulate everything I believed in. The simplicity of our life appeared to crash upon the shoreline rocks of fate.

Teams of doctors, psychologists, counselors and social workers quickly buzzed around my child, finding comparisons to the criteria for an Asperger's diagnosis. (See Appendix A in the back of the book to read more about the DSM IV criteria).

Since then I have gained a wealth of information that has brought me to a conclusion I would never have expected. I now feel the challenge of Asperger's (which I no longer consider a disability), has offered each of our family to grow in hugely beneficial directions. We not only have a deeper appreciation of the choices we make day to day, but are more forgiving of our own mistakes. In addition, we are more accepting of others, no longer expecting them to fit into the comfortable roles we may have envisioned. We take little for granted and take the time to explore more fully each new experience in life. Smiles, laughter and well-being are more important to us than whether or not we are approved of. We live, we laugh, and we love...and we like it that way.

Life is good.

14

Chapter 1

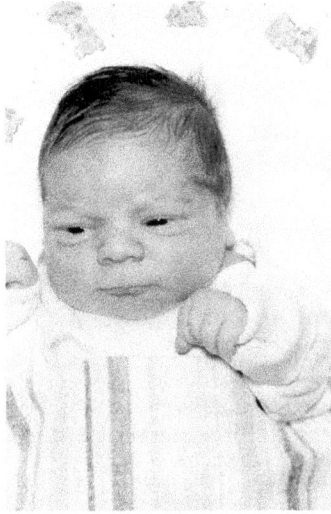

Dual Bottles

I didn't know at first that he was a dragon. When he was born, he looked more like a small gremlin; a dark tuft of fur on top of his head, long squinty eyes, a rather large mouth, and short little legs that bowed at the knees.

I wasn't even sure he'd survived the trip, as a nurse whisked him away before he made a sound.

They returned him shortly and I took inventory of fingers and toes. I remember thinking to myself he looked so different from my first two children I wondered if someone was going to come back into the room, letting me know they had accidentally mixed him up with another baby in the nursery.

He was still silent as he opened his huge dark eyes, which seemed to look right through me.

We bonded. Or perhaps I did, but it didn't really matter.

I worried a little about his silence, but I shouldn't have. As it turned out, he voiced a lot through babyhood.

I would walk and rock him throughout the night, trying to quiet his wails. For that matter, I walked and rocked him through the day too. It was hard not to cry along.

The tone of his wailing was monotone and grating, like a piano in need of tuning. It was difficult to decipher his cries, wondering if he was hungry, tired, or needed his diaper changed, The pitch was always on the same off-key note. Other than his general unhappiness, he really didn't seem that different than other infants, just a bit colicky.

But then, he began to act more like a dragon. He stopped crying and began secluding himself in a cave. A cave with a hidden door.

He wouldn't look at anyone, even when we spoke to him, but would simply stare at objects instead. It was as though the rest of us didn't exist.

We ran him through hearing tests, thinking perhaps he might be somewhat deaf, but the doctors assured me his hearing was fine.

Eventually I got down on my hands and knees and stared into his eyes. He blinked and stared back. The large mouth curled slightly at the corners.

We said hello.

Soon, he went back to batting at the roly-poly jingling duck on the floor next to him.

Abruptly, he stopped waking me up in the night with his cries when he was almost 9 months old. The first night it happened I ran into his room in the morning, terrified the crib-death demons had taken him.

He lay there, staring at Mickey Mouse® on the mobile spinning above his bed.

The crying was apparently over, and I had hopes he was beginning to notice the rest of the world around him.

His sister Brittany, older by 15 months, was now the more demanding of the two. She was learning about the world and wanted to show us everything. She would hold out her arms, begging to be picked up, bring us books to be read aloud, and chattering disjointed toddler phrases constantly.

18

When she failed to get my attention, she turned to Brendan.

"Baby boy, when are you going to talk to me?" When she didn't get an answer, she reached over and grabbed his hand. He squeezed her fingers and kicked his legs at the abrupt invasion of his world. But he didn't let go.

"Smile, baby boy, smile!" she tried next.

"Are you almost ready to come and play yet?" adding, "...we could make sandcastles in the sandbox."

He held onto to her hand with his little fist, almost as if he had decided he needed that small hand more than anything else in the world, and clung to it.

She became his navigator and his connection to the world. Whenever she tried to let go he began to cry. So most of the time...she hung on.

In the car, their car seats had to be buckled in next to each other so he could reach her or he would start to cry. This would make her very upset, and she would demand they be placed closer together. She became very protective.

After breakfast each morning, she would go to play with her dollhouse. As she moved the small doll figures around in the little house, he would scooch his little body inside the miniature walls and fall asleep while he waited for her to finish.

In the afternoon, they would lie next to each other on the floor, holding hands, each sucking from their bottles with their individual rhythms. He would stare up at his bottle, intent on the bubbles rising as his breath replaced the milk. Unaware of most things around him, he seemed extremely aware of his own actions, including the bubbles he'd made.

Brittany would watch him, pulling her bottle away from her mouth long enough to tell him what they were going to do next. She would pop it back into her mouth again, quickly drinking until the bottle squeaked dry, finally throwing it aside. He would simply continue his own slow suckling, still watching the bubbles gently rise.

"Hurry up, baby boy," she would prompt.

Eventually his empty bottle would squeak; then begin to hiss. Sitting up, she would reach over and pull it from his lips with a pop, then toss it in the direction of her own.

Rolling himself over like an overturned turtle, he soon realized he was going to have to get up and follow her if he wanted to continue to share her company; as her energy and curiosity called her back into exploring the world around her.

I tried to show him how to crawl. I would tuck his little knees underneath him, hoping he would understand and shuffle along to a destination. I assumed he would be eager to be mobile as soon as he knew how to do it, like my girls had been.

He would drop back onto the floor, agitated, which in turn would aggravate Brittany.

"Mom, you made him cry."

She would turn around and scowl at me with her rosy little cheeks, auburn curls tossing Shirley Temple-like around her face as she pouted her disapproval where he couldn't see it. "It's OK, baby boy, she still loves you," she would croon.

She reached out The Hand, and he grabbed onto it, pulling himself to his feet next to her.

Within days, they were going almost everywhere together, though he still wouldn't crawl. He refused to put his knees down on the carpet, simply pushing into a downward-dog yoga position when we attempted to help him try. I worried a little about his immature bones bowing under the weight of his body as he gallantly toddled along behind her.

But mostly I was simply glad he didn't cry anymore.

If he wanted his diaper changed, he just took it off; if he wanted sleep, he would just lie down; and his sister always wanted food before he did, so he never seemed hungry.

They took their baths together. Amazingly, it didn't seem to bother him when she would scream and shriek at the top of her lungs if she found a "fuzzy" floating in the water. He would just sit quietly as if he knew her drama was enough for the both of them.

When summer came, they began to head into the back yard to play.

They would work their way towards the lawn; Brendan still a little wobbly. She would walk slowly, waiting for him to catch up while she cooed encouraging words.

"Let's go play on our car, I'll push you, and you can drive the wheel." She would lean back and close the screen door behind him as they left the house.

Some days, she would push him on the swing. The teeter-totter didn't work out as well for them. He would slide off without notice, paying no heed to her cries of dismay when her butt slammed against the ground. She always forgave him anyway.

She continued her litany of guidance.

"Don't eat the grass, baby boy."

"Come this way, baby boy."

"You're supposed to catch the ball when it comes at you, baby boy; not let it hit you."

One day, watching the big red ball bounce repeatedly off his body, I went out to help him hold out his arms to catch it when she threw it. Eventually, we gave up, as his little hands couldn't seem to open and close to catch it.

"We'll look at pictures in the storybooks then, instead," was her response.

I remember thinking how lucky I was that they worked so blissfully well together.

Brendan continued to travel through childhood following his older sister. When he was diagnosed with Asperger's at age 6, although she was only 8, I made the decision to tell her about his challenge. To me, it was clearly evident Brittany was our best link to him, and since she seemed devoted to keeping that connection, I decided we would work within that framework.

She still teaches him when the world isn't looking, and it sometimes occurs to me to wonder if there was pre-conceived design in her being there to help him fit in to our world. If she didn't have to head out into the world now to find her own way, I suspect he might even be able to soon shimmy under the Limbo rod of normalcy.

Of course, not all Asperger's kids are fortunate enough to have a built-in life-guide. Typically, most will struggle through childhood having neither others who understand them, or are accepting enough of their idiosyncrasies to help guide them through the cookie-cutter society in which we live. Brendan has been one of the lucky ones. Of course, if asked, he would surely disagree with this opinion, as most days he believes it is a giant struggle to coexist with the rest of us, having to accept our low tolerance for differences and our resistance to change.

I, as his Mother, know I am also one of the lucky ones. Not only did I have a built-in role model in his sister, Brittany; but I also had the good fortune of not growing up in a typical world myself.

I believe the most helpful thing a parent can do for their child with AS is to lean down and try to look at the world from their child's eyes, as many of their behaviors are not so very hard to understand from their perspective. Once the norms of society, the instincts common to the human condition, and the manipulations of the ego are stripped away, it is truly as if you are seeing through the eyes of the Asperger's child. If you can shed the viewpoints you are accustomed to, and look there, from this simpler and more innocent perspective, you will have a clearer sense of how your child sees the world. This offers you a great opportunity to help guide them through the doorways they cannot see, and into the places you know they will need to grow into, to help them find a space of learned understanding that allows them to be successful within a community to which they do not often relate.

Tony Attwood, a leading authority on Asperger's Syndrome, advises in order to help the child learn to play and coexist with others, as other children often don't have the patience or understanding to play with them, the parent should take an active playmate role with their child.

If the child with AS has a tolerant sibling with whom they bond, as was the case with my children, this bond can offer not only a playmate, but create a bridge where age-appropriate social behaviors can be modeled.

It is important to let siblings know of the difficulties the AS brother or sister faces, and carefully explain how they can help their sibling interact with others at school and with friends, without being a protector.

I would make a side note here, although I found value in utilizing the connection siblings may have, as a parent I would caution how much the other child is leaned upon for this teaching. It can become too easy to make the older child feel responsible for the behaviors of the younger child, which can create issues in the "teaching" sibling's development. I feel it is important to structure balanced time where the children are apart, and to be sure the "teacher" has ample opportunity to be a child in their own peer group. Having Brittany's help in navigating Brendan through childhood meant I had to also be more careful to monitor her progress through her own peer group, as she became mature in her understanding of the psychology of people so quickly it became important she not see her peers as immature. Thankfully, I can report she seems to have grown into a well-balanced, intuitive, sensitive, cheerful and socially dynamic young woman, complete with a confident smile.

There is another reason I would call myself "lucky" to have a child with Aspergers. There is truly great joy to be found in continuously being able to explore and view the world from the childlike perspective the child with Asperger's presents, unencumbered by the guilt of "correct" behavior. How very fortunate to find in every day a fresh idea or viewpoint; to be a child enthralled with finding out why a sky is blue rather than accepting it just "is". If you are the parent of a child with Asperger's, you understand my reference. If you are a parent who has not experienced an AS child, look back to the smiles and feelings of pleasure you experienced when your own toddler explored new things for the first time. Asperger's parents get to enjoy this feeling long after those years are gone. In this sense, we are truly the lucky ones.

In truth, it is rather heart-wrenching to watch and wait fruitlessly for developmental milestones to be met, eventually having to accept they may never come to pass without further intervention and teaching. Motor skills generally mastered during the toddler years often take more time to develop, which I will elaborate on later in this book.

Another thing missing in the experience of raising an Asperger's toddler is the unconditional adoration a parent generally receives from their young child. Waiting for your child's arms to wrap around your neck for a hug can be a painful experience for the parent of a toddler with Asperger's. But as the parent of a teen with Asperger's can attest, the hugs often just happen later than most. The wait can be well rewarded, as my son of 18 will prove by impulsively grabbing me up in a hug with no thought to what his peers might think. No other 18 year-old boy I know will do that in public without persuasion. In my experience, it's simply an unexpected, but balanced trade-off.

Not to mention, the hug is like no other. Randomly given, without thought to position or comfort. It even has a name. We call it "the Brendan hug." When you get one, you know it's his, even if he sent it through someone else.

Chapter 2

Elephant Legs

We wove our grocery cart through the pasta aisle, my toddler Brittany pointing at the Spaghettios, strategically placed on the shelf where they would be caught by the gaze of shopping cart passengers.

"Daddy always makes us Spaghettios, Mama, why can't we get some for your house?" she asked.

"Mama only likes homemade spaghetti, but Daddy likes the canned kind," I answered.

The checkout lane was nearly in front of us.

"Can we get candy?"

"Not today." I replied.

Her younger brother Brendan stared at the candy bars with big brown eyes, belatedly slow in reaching out to snatch one from the impulse rack as we pulled up to the cashier.

"No, Brendan," I said absentmindedly, while trying to get into position to unload the cart. He glanced down at the front of the cart towards Brittany, who was sitting in the basket with the groceries. His little hand still hung out in front of him.

"Elephant legs," he said as his hand swung towards the lady standing in line in front of us, his finger pointing at her ankles.

"Shhh..." I tried to quiet him, embarrassed the woman may have heard his comment.

"But she has wrinkles all around her feet, just like the elephants," he went on" ...and her ankles are HUGE." He was pointing at the folds of baggy nylon stockings bunched above the tops of her Dr. Scholl's, accentuated by the sheer size of her rather large calves.

Brittany's eyes got big as she stared in amazement at her brother's lack of tact.

The lady's head swung around and she gave me a pointed look as if she thought I might need to be reminded of the rudeness of the comments coming from the kid's shopping cage.

"Brendan! That's not a nice thing to say," I admonished.

"But they do look like elephant feet, Mama! See the wrinkles?"

For a brief moment, I wondered if he would be quiet if I gave him the candy bar. Responsible parenting took over.

"We will talk about it later Brendan. Right now I need you to be quiet, because I have to pay for the groceries."

The lady harrumphed in front of us. I was afraid it might elicit another comment from Brendan, as she sounded a little more like a horse than an elephant right at the moment, but he had gone back to pointing at the candy bars, and thankfully was not paying her any more attention.

Brittany slyly looked down at the lady's feet, being careful not to let the woman catch her looking.

I was cautious not to hurry the woman with the cart, trying to avoid the animosity I could feel rippling back through the checkout lane.

Thankfully, Elephant Lady stomped out the door before the situation could get any worse.

On the way home in the car we tried to have a "nice people never do this" talk, but it was very hard to keep it black and white.

I eventually gave up trying to make him understand, realizing the more I tried to explain, the less rational my arguments seemed to him. To Brendan, truth was truth, and that was that.

When an elementary school counselor first suggested Brendan be evaluated for Asperger's Syndrome, I ordered Tony Attwood's book by the same name. As I began to read through the chapters, it was as though he had been meeting with my child in secret, writing down all of the funny mannerisms and quirky behaviors Brendan displays. Initially, I laughed off the coincidences, reminding myself how easy it is to fit characteristics to horoscopes, or neurotically add up medical symptoms to fit a disease. It didn't take long however, to realize the proverbial nail had been hit on the head. In one of his books, I found a description of a scene that was almost identical to the one we had experienced.

Years later, after he was diagnosed, I realized there were likely going to be many similar moments in our life, where I would need to find ways to quickly educate the "injured" about Brendan's differences, as teaching Brendan accepted social etiquette was likely to take quite some time.

A child with Asperger's, having a limited set of social skills, will often not only embarrass others, but also fail to feel any remorse for their comments. Their lack of empathy is not an evidence of a cruel or apathetic nature, but rather a non-understanding of the personal and sometimes emotional impact of their words. As they have not generally considered how their words will be received, they tend to speak directly from their train of thought.

This trait also makes them very honest as a rule, especially when they are youngsters. Complete honesty is typical in the younger child with Asperger's. As many of our behaviors are designed to protect the ego, often through the use of "little white lies", this trait contributes to the child being perceived as odd by not only their peers, but adults as well.

Generally, they do not learn to lie until they begin to observe others, and recognize dishonesty. This doesn't happen as early as most children, as children with Asperger's do very little observing of other's behaviors. As they are taught and learn to model these behaviors, they gain the skill of manipulation, which is typically learned early in childhood.

Once they begin to learn appropriate behavior, they often take the teaching so to heart they begin to try to correct others, seeing their behaviors as "wrong". Rules can become very black and white. It is important to explain the difference between being an observer when the situation does not call for interference, and listening to their inner voice when speaking up would be the correct response. Kind of like walking a tightrope. It's all about balance.

Allowing them to use their newly acquired understanding of "correct" behavior to monitor situations with their peers, will only serve to set them even further apart.

Therefore, sometimes it may become necessary to intercede when the child with Asperger's confronts other children about their behaviors, as their drive to police the situation is generally much stronger than their desire to create friendships.

The AS child has difficulty interpreting other people's vocal cues, body language and expectations, so they often react to situations very directly and inappropriately.

The very nature of social cues, vary from person to person. Body language, tone of voice, mannerisms, and even personal style, make it difficult for these children to interpret these signals. They find it far easier to deal with concrete concepts with clear conclusions. Science and math are easier than the sociology of relationships to someone with Asperger's.

Most Asperger's research agrees this difficulty with social interaction is the most obvious characteristic of Asperger's. AS children tend to be very self-centered and internally focused, finding it extraordinarily difficult to see things from any viewpoint but their own. Even once they mature enough to understand how they might benefit by adjusting their behavior, their efforts can be awkward at best.

Methods of teaching social skills are now being used with these children while in their formative years to assist them with fitting in to mainstream society. *Social Stories*, a procedure developed by Carol Gray, which consists of giving the child written social situations and then helping them decipher the unspoken meanings within them, are a beneficial way of educating those with Asperger's. Studies show the child with Asperger's is able to grasp these concepts, provided they are taught in a deductive manner, i.e. a smile equals satisfaction and a frown equals dissatisfaction. The difficulty lies in making social cues fit into black and white categories, as the "gray areas" make it very difficult to show distinct patterns. Slight hints such as tone of voice which we may pick up on, can make the same situation nearly impossible to decipher from an Asperger's perspective.

Additional social skills training, provided to Brendan by counselors, were one of the most helpful treatments used to help him with overcoming this obstacle. Body language lessons given at home, along with after-school discussions with his sister Brittany about the day's interactions with other kids, have all helped make this most common of Asperger's traits nearly non-existent in Brendan.

I now believe these kids just don't instinctively read the body language of people as most toddlers do, so they don't make the connections at any early age. They are so caught in their own worlds they don't naturally absorb the mannerisms of those around them. We are so used to typical development where toddlers intuitively learn to influence people to get what they desire; when we come across a child who does not have that intuition, we often fail to recognize they just need direction in the process. By directly teaching them how to "read" people, I believe most can quite easily become adept enough at social maneuvering to make their way.

With Brendan, we played face games when he was young to help teach him how to make facial expressions and body language to display emotions and moods. Admittedly, most of his facial emotes are theatrical and over-stated, often earning him place in the theatre and drama clubs. I still have to remind him his expressions of more vivid emotions, such as anger, head over the appropriately acceptable line more often than I would like, but to his credit, his face will generally adjust at the reminder.

Most adults who meet him now think he is just a well-mannered, intelligent, and slightly geeky teenager. Little do they know that he has simply been taught to only whisper "Elephant Legs" under his breath, rather than speaking it aloud.

Happiness/excitement

Chapter 3

Mini-Man

Brittany was gearing up for kindergarten, and was determined she was going to know how to read before she went. After dinner one evening, while I was helping her with phonetics, Brendan climbed up next to us on the couch.

"How do you read?" he asked.

I hesitated for a moment, trying to put it into words that would make sense for someone just about to turn 3.

"Well..." I began, "You take the sounds I've been teaching Sissy about the alphabet letters, and put them together to make words. Like b...a...t..." I sounded out the letter and then slowly pronounced it, the way I recalled learning as a child.

He glanced at a word on the book in my lap, and then interrupted my explanation. "What's the sound for 'D'?" he asked. We repeated the process for "O" and "G".

It was his turn to hesitate.

"Dog" he said.

"Very good!" I will admit I was a little impressed, but at the moment wrote it off to either maternal pride or just plain luck.

He reached over and grabbed another of the library books I had just brought home for his sister. I knew he had never heard me read this particular book, so I was sure he would give up quickly, shortening our conversation and allowing me to get back to helping his sister with her studies.

By then, I should have known better. He didn't even take the time to sound out each letter and then slowly cement the sounds back into a word like his sister would have. He simply sat... studied the next word in the book...and then blurted them out with monotone precision. No sign of excitement or pride in his accomplishment was evident in either his voice or his words.

I couldn't hold out with my own sense of humility. *My boy*, though he may have seemed a little slow out of the gate, had illustrated that my dream of having exceptional children was again coming true. It was now a certainty mine were brilliant; I was one of the "lucky Moms." *This child* could read before the age of three.

Though I realized his apparent genius was not truly a result of my parenting efforts, at that moment I was still exceptionally proud I could claim the title of "Mom".

Here was the child that didn't take any work to teach, he just absorbed information by osmosis through his sister. Teach one...you taught them both.

I beamed down into the little face that showed no pride.

"Very, very good, Brendan."

He blinked at me, picked up another book, and turned back to his room.

After that, we took turns reading the bedtime story.

The Big Apple
Award given to

Brendan Townsend

for

being a reading
group hot shot !

The Big Apple
Award given to

Brendan Townsend

for

being a reading
group wonder !

The next day, Brendan brought me the newspaper, and pointed to the word *astronaut*, pronouncing it clearly. Within weeks, he could read almost anything, though I'm certain he couldn't possibly understand everything he was reading due to his lack of maturity.

One of the things most noticeably different about toddlers with Asperger's, is when they finally begin to speak, often later than most, their language is very precise, and spoken with each word and sound pronounced very distinctly. Most toddlers piece together nouns and verbs, leaving out many of the conjunctive terms at first, primarily trying to get their point across: i.e. "Doggie run" or "Mama working". The child with Asperger's often seem almost to hold off until they understand the structure of grammar and then burst out with an adult-like repertoire.

This manner of speaking is commonly referred to as pedantic in descriptions of children with AS. I've commonly heard the condition of AS itself referred to as "Little Professor Syndrome", largely because of this trait. Here in the United States, where the English language has become a grab bag of slang terms and contractions, their speech patterns often make them stand out against other children in school. Although adults may find their methods of speech charming and proper, their peers often see it as just another basis for ridicule. The words they choose when speaking often sound stilted and formal. Rather than developing the slang curve most of us speak with, they sound more like a reference book.

Their tone may lack empathy as well, often not matching the expectations of the person they're speaking to. This also makes them prime targets for not only peer bullying, but can get them into hot water quickly with adults in authority. Adults in charge may not understand it is likely they're not trying to be disrespectful, but rather that these kids do not travel the usual language pathways.

Miscommunication can be exacerbated by the fact that nearly everything said to a child with Asperger's is often taken quite literally. As such, euphemisms are lost, and sarcasm is generally not understood, in part due to their difficulty in differentiating tone of voice.

One of my early memories of young Brendan was his desire to decipher acronyms, once I'd explained how they were used. Simply seeing capital letters put together would lead him down a mental path to determine what the letters represented. I don't recall ever thinking about the origin of the letters ATM until one day when we pulled up in front of one, with Brendan piping up from his car seat to say, "That is an Automatic Teller Machine. It replaces the bank teller in the window when she has to go home at night." This came after a discussion about employees not actually living in stores and banks.

Much of the life of these youngsters is dedicated to absorbing bits and pieces of data rather than trying to learn from the people around them; the usual way for young children to gather information.

Those with Asperger's often exhibit what is commonly referred to as a photographic memory. Although this is not necessarily a trait limited to those with AS, it seems to be widespread across this group.

Brendan not only can quote back from pages in a book, and memorize poems with ease, but can watch someone play a piano piece, and then play it himself, although he has only had a couple of piano lessons. His instructor told me after purchasing scores for him to tutor with, that after the first time he played them I might as well throw the music away, as he never looked at it a second time.

Using this characteristic to their benefit, they often exhibit high levels of rote intelligence, perhaps from this tendency to absorb visual data.

This is especially common within their area of interest, which they can often recite verbatim from data they have read. As is discussed more in Chapter 9, it is a marker of AS when a child has an absorbing interest in one particular subject, often to the exclusion of wanting to learn about anything else. For many AS kids, the subjects are mechanical or scientific in nature, and very detailed. Astronomy, trains, and engineering are examples of typical Asperger's passions. I believe this may be in part due to the nature of the information written about these subjects, as the technical format generally used when describing these subjects is clear and concise, making it relatively easy for their minds to absorb.

On the other hand, auditory information is often lost as quickly as the next words are heard. Without a visual marker to connect the memory with, words and sounds seem more difficult to retain. Personally, I wonder if this has a connection to the fact that those with Asperger's shut out some auditory input during conscious hours, in order to relieve the stress of processing a multitude of tones they are uncomfortable with.

Although I have never been evaluated for Asperger's, I see many of the characteristics in myself. I also not only have a photographic memory, and the ability to see in my mind where I have put something in order to retrieve it later, but I also have a terrible time with remembering things spoken to me, particularly sequences of information. There are more similarities, but girls born in my era grew up with a different set of rules.

Even now, girls with AS are quite often left undiagnosed due to the differences in cultural expectations for our gender. Although boys are expected to bond together in social situations such as sports, many girls who are independent and quiet are simply taken as "bookworms", and are accepted much more easily despite their anomolies.

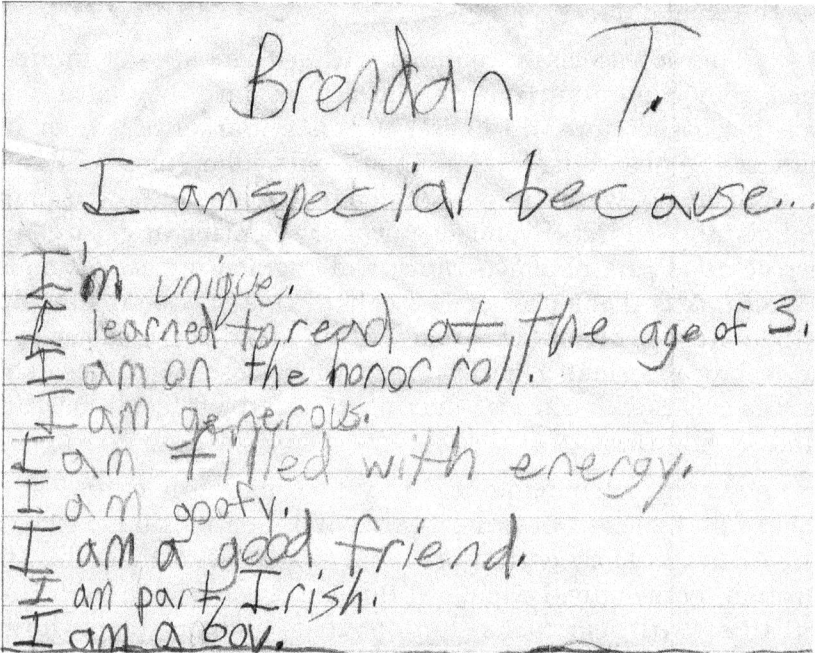

Brendan T.

I am special because...

I'm unique.

I learned to read at the age of 3.

I am on the honor roll.

I am generous.

I am filled with energy.

I am goofy.

I am a good friend.

I am part Irish.

I am a boy.

Chapter 4

The Short Bus

By the time Brendan turned 4, it was exceedingly apparent he was awkward at playing with other children. It wasn't simply that he wasn't good at sharing, too aggressive, or too timid to talk to the other kids. Most of the time he simply didn't seem to notice them, and when he did, he would look at them quizzically, as though they were merely small bits of foreign matter that made funny noises.

Pre-school seemed like it might be a good place for him to learn to interact with others. He was so full of creative energy, I thought he would do well spreading finger paint around on big sheets of paper with the other children, perhaps making friendships in the process. It seemed to me this type of environment might be exactly where he would begin to blend in with other children.

So, on a crisp September morning, we stood at the end of the driveway, with me holding his small hand in case he decided to dart out in front of the bus. He stood calmly next to me, showing no apprehension or, to be honest, the excitement I had hoped for. Soon a short yellow bus pulled up with a squeak of the brakes all buses seem to have. Walking him to the door as it swung open, the first step seemed a little too high for his short legs to manage, so I lifted him a little to reach it before letting go of his hand. He didn't turn around to wave, but simply disappeared into the darkness of the bus as he rounded the top step.

The bus motor rumbled quietly for a few moments. I pictured his small body making his way to the back of the bus, where we always sat together when we rode the city buses. Finally, the bus pulled away, but I continued to stand there for a moment. My youngest child had now traveled off into the world without me to guide him. I stood there with the distressful feeling of things left undone.

Shaking it off, and laughing at myself a bit for my maternal musings, I returned to the house.

Less than an hour later, long before even telemarketers were awake, the phone rang. Apprehensively, I dropped the book I was reading and picked up the receiver.

"Hello?"

"Hello? Is this Mrs. Townsend? This is the Head Start program calling about your son Brendan..." the woman began. "Brendan seems to be having difficulty with being here, and we thought it best to call you and ask you to come and pick him up.

Oh no, what now?... I thought.

"He seemed fine when he got on the bus. What's happened?" I asked.

"Well, it was actually the bus driver who reported the first problem," she continued. "He apparently attacked her. She said he cannot ride her bus again, and you will need to provide transportation to the program from now on. We tried to calm him down, but he just isn't settling in well at all here either. He simply screams if we try to guide him to an activity. Truthfully, we don't think our program is the right place for him."

I hung up the phone, and got in the car to pick him up. One of the teachers opened the door, murmuring a quick, "Thank you for coming," as I walked in. Brendan was sitting in a chair by the door with his coat on, staring intently at his feet swinging under the seat. The sounds of other children, excited by the pictures they were creating, drifted into the hallway from an adjacent classroom.

"Hey, Bren, how are you doing?" I asked as I squatted down in front of his chair to look at his face.

"I don't like it here. They try to restrain me," he replied as he glared angrily towards the teacher.

The teacher quickly chimed in "The bus driver tried to buckle him into a seat belt. It is a requirement all of the students wear a seat belt on the bus for their safety. She said he just started screaming and would not let her buckle him. He bit her."

At once, I could see my folly. Brendan had ridden school buses before when we took a field trip with his sister's class, but the other buses had no seatbelts. A padded toddler seat was the only restraint he was accustomed to, and he'd never ridden anywhere with a stranger in charge. I knew from experience Brendan did not do well with things out of his ordinary routine. He didn't like change, and I'd always verbally tried to prepare him for new things. I knew when things came at him too fast he would panic, and I'd not taken the possibilities that came with these new routines into consideration.

I made a mental note to call tomorrow and explain, but could see neither of them was willing to try and resolve the matter at the moment. The teacher was wringing her hands, looking frustrated and slightly exhausted, though it was still early morning. Brendan simply went back to staring at his swinging feet.

"Thank you for calling; sorry about the difficulty." I grabbed Brendan's hand and led him towards the exit.

"Good luck," the teacher called after us.

Those with Asperger's Syndrome often experience distressful anxiety when dealing with new situations, or breaking from their usual routines. Even as infants, they tend to deal better when a routine structure of daily tasks is developed. These patterns are generally easier for them to remember, helping them with learning responsibility for self-care such as tooth-brushing and showering. This sort of structure can mean the difference between a child who needs continual instruction in basic tasks, and one who can take responsibility for their own self-care. Because they find it easier to remember things without variables, the ability to remember learned behaviors is constructed by developing a simple routine for the tasks they need to be able to do on a daily basis.

My son had difficulty with choosing clothes for school when he would awake in the morning, often missing the school bus after running out of time. We began a routine where he would choose what he was going to wear the following day before he went to bed each night. His stress in the morning was considerably lessened by this one simple change. As an added bonus, the humor in my day began when I would see his clothes arranged like a small person on the floor, as if the child wearing them had simply disappeared from within. It was hard to keep a smile off my face each morning when I would open his bedroom door to wake him for school.

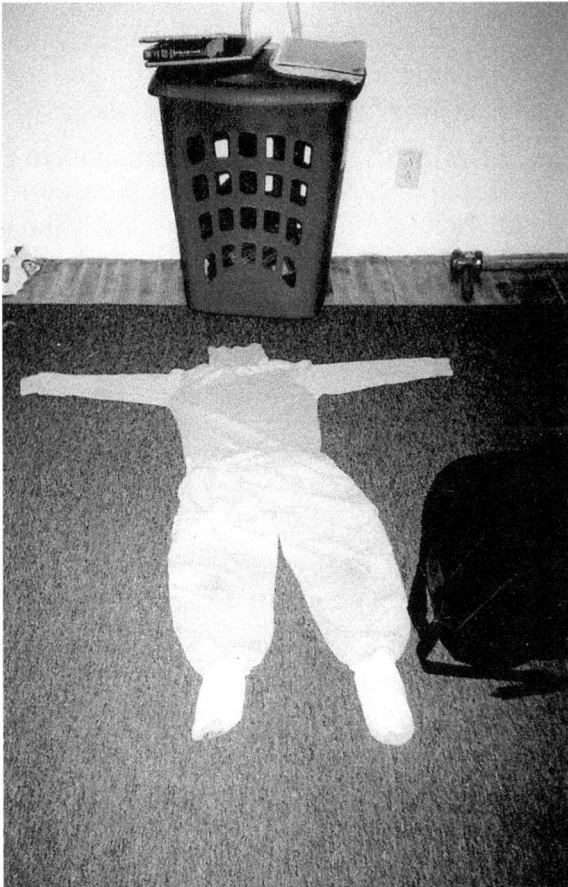

I might also add that later, as the child becomes older, if these tasks were not made part of a daily routine, there may come a time where the child with AS goes through a phase where they simply quit doing them. This is true of non-AS adolescents as well, but becomes a more difficult situation to deal with for the child with Asperger's. Often, the adolescent with AS goes through a period where they begin to question the relevance of these behaviors; i.e. showering and cleanliness activities. Because they are not as socially connected as the neurotypical child, (which I will hereafter refer to as NT), it can become a difficult debate between parent and child. The parent may need to prioritize the value of enforcing these behaviors against the responsibility of helping the child develop self-esteem. Especially when they are already not being accepted by their peers, regardless of personal hygiene. Being accepted at home can become paramount to avoiding depression.

On the other hand, there is a valid argument in the belief parental management (i.e. control) from this perspective is perhaps a more humane lesson than the struggle with the additional peer pressure an unwashed teen will suffer in school.

I chose the "public" rule. When you're going out in public, you follow "public" rules. At home, we love you regardless.

In my experience, eventually there comes a time when the teenage AS child develops an understanding of why hygienic routines are important. I do promote having a regimented routine developed during early childhood. It can help eliminate the need for justifying the actions to a teen who has begun to question everything the world does. If they have always done something, they are less likely to question doing it.

Another source of anxiety which may cause self-esteem issues, are self-soothing behaviors much like those exhibited in classic autism. These can include flapping repetitive movements, motor tics and verbal or guttural noises. Sometimes these behaviors are referred to as Tourette's Syndrome, which is often found in combination with Asperger's. It has been suggested these verbal and physical behaviors may perhaps be a manner of alleviating the stress they encounter while trying to manage life. Sometimes these movements may even be self-injurious due to their repetitive nature.

These additional challenges can make the AS child even more susceptible to anxiety and depression. Being supportive and understanding by providing an environment where the child can escape to calm and soothe them, can be very helpful.

One of the most helpful things you can do for your child is to alleviate stress they may have encountered during their school day. There are a number of ways to do this, from providing a quiet corner for the child to work in, physical exercise, and more focused treatments such as Brushing.

Brushing was very helpful for my son during his elementary years. The Brushing treatment consists of using a specially designed, soft-bristled brush, which is stroked down the child's arms, legs and back in order to provide sensory stimulation, which in turn stimulates hormone production to the brain. This assisted in slowing Brendan's tics when external and auditory stimulation became overwhelming. The brushing also seemed to help him be more able to adjust to stressful situations, and we additionally would use it at school and home when stressful moments were anticipated. Eventually, he seemed to gain better internal defenses, allowing him to block more of the external stressors. Subsequently, he became less and less dependent on the Brushing as time went on.

I also found it beneficial to remind Brendan the Tourette's type symptoms he was experiencing generally begin to disappear after puberty. This helped Brendan to not let the tics affect his self-esteem, especially when teased by his peers about them. Although they still annoyed him, (and everyone else who might be trying to watch a movie with him), it helped make them less worrisome for all concerned. Now, it is a rare period when Brendan experiences tics at all, and we expect they will soon be gone forever. I only notice them now when he is anxious about formulating a response he knows someone is waiting for. The tics appear to be an automatic response to the impatience he incurs when he lengthily pauses to think.

There are also a number of medications that can be prescribed to help with the anxiety and other symptoms that often present themselves alongside Asperger's. We tried utilizing them for a time; some had good effects, others not so good. In our own personal battle, we decided as a team we would rather face the "real" symptoms as opposed to those symptoms that were by-products of the medications. I also felt it beneficial that Brendan should learn to feel confident in dealing with his condition based on his own reality, in hopes he would be less likely to feel overwhelmed by his Asperger's if the time came in life where he was unable to have access to medications. It was a personal choice to raise him without the benefits of medication, with the alternative available at any time.

Your pediatrician should be able to refer you to the doctors in your area who can help you explore the options of medications so you can make your own personal decisions with regards to your child.

Another calming element for many AS kids is an artistic outlet such as music. Brendan now soothes himself by heading to a piano or organ, where he will spend hours composing or simply plucking out songs he has heard.

A number of ideas from parents of other children with Asperger's are available online. There are a number of websites and web-rings that have been created by parents to help share these pieces of helpful information. Some of the best ideas I have found have come directly from other families who have sought out ways to help their own children. Some of the best opportunities to assist your child will come from these connections.

I've listed some of the resources I found most helpful in the back of this book.

Chapter 5

The Einstein Theory

With a loud *POP,* all the lights in the house went out. A bone-chilling scream sent me running upstairs from the basement where I was framing a photograph. Stubbing my toe in my haste, I dashed up the stairs to check on Brendan and his sister whom I'd left watching television. It was early afternoon, and the kids sat in a small puddle of window-light. The house felt foreign with the silence of nothingness, left behind when the electricity went out. Brittany's tousled curls bobbed up and down angrily, while her eyes stabbed scornful looks at her younger brother. He just sat there, wide-eyed, looking back at her with a totally blank look on his face. His hair stuck up, bed-head and disheveled-looking, much like a miniature Einstein. Actually, it almost always looked this way.

Still, it did look as though he might be in shock. Trying to cut to the quick, I turned back to Brittany. "What happened?"

"Brendan did it."

At least she always gave a normal 6-year-old response to my questions.

"Did what?" My hands flung out in a pleading gesture, impatient for the response so I could get back to dealing with the catatonic one.

"He poked it." she said.

I took a breath and tried to calm myself, knowing that if I pressed her harder it was only going to take longer to find out what was wrong.

"What do you mean...he poked *What?*"

"He stuck the tweezers in the slots and all the lights went off," she went on.

"Tweezers?" Noticing the electrical outlet on the wall, *Safety Mom* pondered on how much brain damage could be done by a solid metal connection to 110 volts. "Did he pass out?"

By the look on her face I was certain I'd lost her. Attempting to rephrase my question, I asked, "Did he go to sleep when he did it and then wake back up again?"

"I don't think so." she replied.

He still stared at us.

I went back to examining him. Although he may have seemed a little more distant than usual, he appeared to be fine.

"Bren?"

His eyes slowly looked up at mine. *This was good.*

"Are you OK? Do you hurt anywhere?"

He shook his head NO.

Duh...Two questions. Now I had to figure out which one he was answering.

"Are you OK?"

He blinked.

"What happened?"

Without hesitation, he held out the pair of tweezers that were in his hand. The once pointed ends were melted inward and scorched.

"Brendaaaaaaan!" The word flew out long and loud, even though I had fully intended to stay calm and collected.

"It was fine," he said, matter-of-factly.

"Fine? What do you mean fine?" It was hard to stay rational when maternal instinct insisted the small human in front of me should have been taking the whole thing much more seriously.

"The tweezers have a rubber handle," he replied. "They won't let the electricity get me." He paused. "Rubber doesn't conduct electricity. You said so."

Not for the first time I had to remind myself he was only five.

Shortly before, I had told them about a childhood friend of mine who almost died from touching an overhead wire with a pole. His rubber-soled tennis shoes saved his life. A sigh escaped me as I realized my folly.

I held out my hand for the experimental tweezers with the now twisted ends. After a moment comprehending what I wanted him to do, he placed them in the palm of my hand.

I wanted to tip him over my knee, give him a spanking the way my Mother would have done, have some certainty the lesson was learned and would not be repeated. I knew it wouldn't work. A spanking would no more stop him from further experimentation than discarding the tweezers would.

Safety Mom jumped out in front of me and waved her finger back and forth in front of the kids. I fought my emotional response...*Think rationally.*

"This was pure luck," I said. "Electricity can jump from one conductive surface to another, and you were the closest thing to ground." I added.

I tried to out-think the mini-geek sitting on the floor in front of me...

"Statistics include the number of times you can complete a dangerous action without having it go in the wrong direction. You've used up a big chance. I would recommend saving the rest, because you might need them later as you are designing inventions...like your ancestors."

I was referring to Edward Jenner, a distant ancestor who invented the smallpox vaccine. Brendan loved the idea he had the mind-stock of someone so inventive. I'd played this card before, and hoped it would work one more time.

"OK".

I stood looking at him, trying to see if the words had made it in.

An idea occurred to me. "Why don't you use the gift certificate you got for Christmas to buy an electrical light kit so you can see how it works?" I suggested.

His eyes lit up a little, like he had just received the gift again.

I'll go get it, it's in my room," he said. The blank look was gone. He bumped into Brittany as he rose, who continued to look down at her toes, apparently still trying to avoid my attention.

Picking my battles, I turned my attention back to Brendan.

"Yes, that's a good idea," I said.

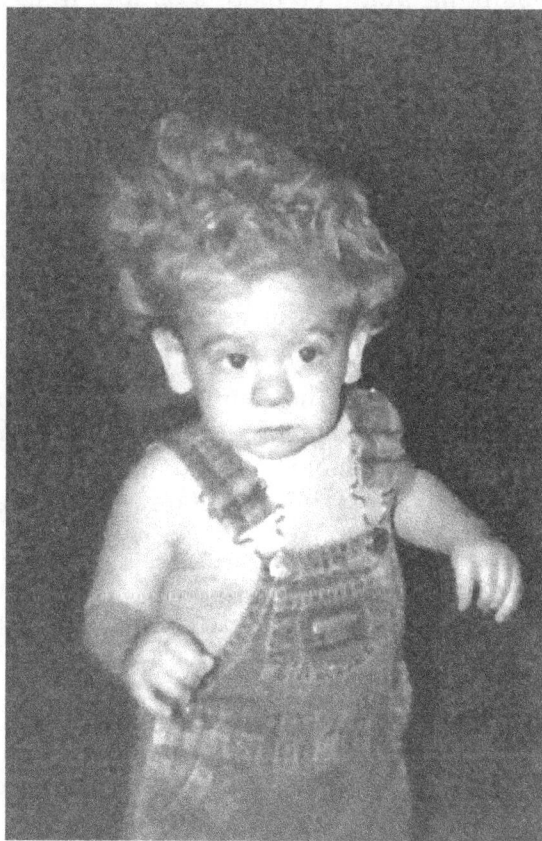

There's a theory Einstein may have had Asperger's. (Grandin 1988) Einstein's well-documented impairment of social skills, along with his genius in creative thinking, suggests he may have simply come before the label, which was not commonly used until 1981.

Having Asperger's syndrome can actually offer a vast array of benefits. As the level of intelligence increases, and the value of conformity diminishes, we become more readily inspired to think freely, producing some of our most genius inventions, music and art. Many of the most famous innovators and philosophers in history have been theorized to have characteristics of Asperger's. Mozart, Ben Franklin, Marie Curie, Picasso, da Vinci, and even Bill Gates have all been referred to as perhaps being on the spectrum.

According to Hans Asperger, this syndrome is linked with mathematical and scientific genius. Asperger claimed, "... for success in science and art, a dash of autism is essential." (Encarta 2009)

I had talked with Brendan how others hadn't understood Einstein's oddities, much like the way people reacted to Brendan himself. I thought the comparison might help him to understand his differences were not necessarily disabilities, but rather simply traits that define the uniqueness of AS individuals. I suggested we had become so "boxed" in our behaviors as an American community, that we now simply produce labels for those who don't fit in those boxes. I hoped if I could get Brendan to understand differences were a part of life's natural design to ensure the continuance of the human species, I could help to counterbalance the less than beneficial remarks he was going to encounter from those who might not be so cautious with his self-esteem.

I perceived my actions as helping him develop self-confidence in a society unlikely to accept many of his behaviors, since they were often so far outside the norm. Convincing him he was "specialized" rather than "disabled" seemed to be an excellent way to accomplish this.

All actions having an equal reaction, he took my bolstering to mean he was simply better than the norm. In his mind, the rest of us became average citizens who could be counted as sheep-like creatures who accepted conformity, summarily dismissing us as lesser beings.

He was 4 when he decided he was smarter than the rest humanity. Admittedly, I hadn't counted on being included in the "rest of us".

In a conversation about people with unique thought patterns, we talked about Einstein's theories of energy, and how we now used his own brilliance to light our homes. As the previous story suggests, with these kids, it can be important to consider the continuation of linear thought when presenting new information.

Of course, as a mom, I had warned both the toddlers about the dangers of electrical sockets, explaining the power inside them could stop the human heart in an instant.

The conversations were far apart, and I had kept them simple as I was explaining to toddlers. But I had forgotten to take into consideration Brendan wasn't 4 intellectually.

His testing of the theory electricity would flow through the tweezers, leaving him unharmed because of the rubber handles, yet leaving his sister in total amazement of his genius was a splicing of bits of information he had learned from me.

It was so simple; I had trouble believing I hadn't seen it. It was as plain as the melted tweezers he held in his hand.

Chapter 6

The Ramp

A white bike helmet perched atop his head, Brendan zipped up and down the hill of the gravel driveway on his new two-wheeler bicycle. The helmet was my idea. He wanted no part of it. I still wasn't able to let go of the *Safety Mom* mode with him, though he was ten and certainly capable of riding a bike on our rural driveway. Actually, I wasn't sure I would be comfortable letting him ride on the highway out front of our house before he was thirty.

Taking one last glance out the kitchen window, I turned and went into the living room to fold towels. Sheryl Crow crooned power-chick music on the radio. I found the beat energizing; it was just the type of music I usually chose for mundane chores like housework and laundry.

While folding, I dreamily admired the flowers in the field out the window. Daisies and purple coneflowers danced in the sun, happy to coexist with the native milkweeds. I hadn't been able to make myself till the field under and uproot the natural wild beauty growing there, so each year I just threw in whatever seeds I could find.

The teapot began to sing in the kitchen, its high soprano note nearly harmonizing with Sheryl's throaty voice.

I stepped back into the kitchen, flipping off the stove burner and turning to the tea cupboard. My eyes caught a glimpse of Brendan facing towards the barn, hunched low over the handlebars, intent upon a ramp, which headed up into the barn's doorway.

The world dropped into slow motion as he put both feet on the bike pedals.

Visualizing the stacks of glass windows I knew were leaning just inside the barn door, I fumbled with the window latches, hastily trying to turn them the right way. On the second try I ripped open the sash, hearing the tearing of last winter's weather-stripping as I flung the window wide.

"Brendannnnnnnn....Nooooooo!!!"

Time nearly stopped.

His pace slowed as the brakes took charge, making it worth the extra charge I had paid to have them adjusted by the Toys-R-Us assembly department.

My heart rate slowed along with the bike. He put his feet down on the ramp just as the bike crested the doorway, turning around to look blankly back at me.

Motioning for him to come inside, I shut the window, mentally noting I would need to clean off the weather-stripping residue before it stained the woodwork.

The Asperger's Syndrome child generally has difficulty with grasping the concepts of cause and effect without mentoring. NT children seem to gather this knowledge during the reward-driven experiences of toddlerhood. The child with AS has difficulty recognizing these patterns, since individual situations vary in their structure. This often leaves them less able to predict results of their actions.

There are a couple of primary reasons those with AS have such difficulty learning from previous situations. Few teaching experiences are summarily black or white. A simple variable can change the result from good to bad, in nearly the exact same circumstances. Ramps are made for jumping on bikes. It takes speed to jump a ramp. (Not all ramps are safe for bikes.) It can be difficult for those with AS to predict variations. Their minds are so data organized, in order to anticipate results, it seems they must have experienced each individual outcome in an exactly similar sequence of events.

The other obstacle is they often haven't considered the chain of events from beginning to end before they do something. They don't think ahead.

This has been one of the ongoing lessons that continues to occur with Brendan. Since each new situation is a unique opportunity to learn, we try to keep a running dialogue to help him understand the directions his decisions might take him. This is true with all parenting, but I believe the difference lies in the need for the verbal reminder to evaluate choices. I don't have to remind my other children to look for cars coming. I remind Brendan to think ahead, a lot.

I remember Brendan being fascinated with the concept of an action having a reaction; building massive domino villages, each piece reacting with the next. I also think in retrospect, that games such as "Mousetrap", where cause and effect were made visual, could have been aids in developing a better understanding.

I believe this difficulty with understanding the relationships between cause and effect also contributes to their slow development of motor skills. It takes a clear understanding of the dynamics, to choose our reactions before the action happens. Catching a ball may seem simple, but calculating and performing the steps necessary to be in the proper position to do so, can be challenging to someone on the AS spectrum. Brendan and I gave up on playing ball for just this reason; as every time I managed to get the ball close to him, it would just hit him before he could put his hands up to catch it. Eventually, we changed direction, and stuck with rolling the ball back and forth.

For Asperger's kids, these motor skills are often difficult to grasp, and slow in the making. Their social awkwardness, combined with lessened motor skills, makes it hard to join into games with other school mates. They generally find themselves in the last group of children chosen as teammates in sports.

The difficulty with fine motor skills is often exhibited in poor or stilted handwriting. Brendan has some of the most unusual handwriting I have witnessed, although it can be clearly read, it has a visual appearance similar to the manner in which he speaks.

This eccentricity is not due to difficulty with language skills, as he is very proficient at learning other languages. From sign language to French, to the ability to read and write fluently in Anglo-Saxon runes (which he has taught himself). Below is the phrase, "I am a dragon", written by Brendan, in Anglo-Saxon runes.

ᛁ ᛗᛗ ᚠ ᛞᚱᚠᚷᛗᚾ

Another characteristic of many children with Asperger's is their hyper-mobility. Double-jointedness is common, and their bodies can be extremely flexible. Logical reasoning suggests it is harder for them to gain control of their bodies in part due to this extra range of motion. Much like the selection tool in photo editing programs, it is easier to control the action of one that snaps to a grid, than a free-form tool, which needs greater direction from the user.

Patient teaching of simple motor skills such as rolling and catching a ball can help with their development. Creating shapes with clay or scissors is another great tool. Practice makes perfect. As siblings generally don't have the patience needed to teach, it is advised for an adult to work with the child one on one to develop proficiency.

Play dates, or putting the child together with other children with Asperger's, helps to give them a place where their own skills can seem typical, offering opportunities for raised self-esteem. These play dates also offer better chances for peer acceptance, which the Asperger's youngster lacks. Though it may seem like there is little connection between children during playtime, it still offers beneficial skills in cooperation, and simply being in the company of peers.

One of the strategies for helping Brendan to develop social skills was to have him join peer groups such as Boy Scouts of America, and extracurricular group activities such as Little League Baseball. From our own experience, we found Brendan not only found these experiences non-rewarding due to his social and motor difficulties, but they simply added to his feelings of peer inadequacy. Time spent with children either much older or much younger than himself seemed to help more. He was able to connect on an intellectual level more easily with mature students. With younger children, he was able to help guide them, which made him feel good about himself.

The motor skills challenges were surmountable, and I am happy to say that although Brendan still exhibits some awkwardness, he has fine-tuned the mastery of his physical body to an art form many would envy. A few of my co-workers, ballet dancers nonetheless, have stood and watched astounded while Brendan tucked one leg disjointedly up behind his shoulder, and stood on the other while juggling three balls into the air and whistling a tune. Now that's special.

Chapter 7

Heat in the Cheeks

"Brendannnnn...dinner's ready!"

I shouted our usual one-minute warning from the kitchen, knowing he could hear me through the wall adjoining his bedroom. Continuing to set dishes on the table, I stomped three times on the floor to his sister, which was her signal to come upstairs.

Within minutes, the rest of the family was gathered around the table, but Brendan's chair still sat empty. I went over and opened his bedroom door, looking inside and finding the room empty as well.

"Anyone know where Bren is?" I asked.

A chorus of "No's" came from the dinner table.

Weird, I thought. He'd been here just a little bit ago when I'd given him a bath before dinner. I thought maybe he'd fallen asleep in his closet, where he sometimes liked to sit and read to the new litter of kittens, so I went back into his room, closing the door in order to get to the closet behind it.

Catching me by surprise, Brendan stood there just behind the door, looking at the floor. His navy blue footie-jammies hung down unzipped around his tummy. He looked a little like a doll dropped in the midst of play.

"Bren?" I leaned down and tipped to see his face.

He looked at me with his giant eyes.

"Dinner's ready. Are you coming?"

"My butt hurts," he replied.

"I'm sorry, let's see if we can fix it." I grabbed his hand to lead him to the bathroom. Seafood fettucini wasn't much good cold, and I hoped to get us to the table before congealment. His feet stayed stuck to the floor.

"Did you have a big number two?" I asked, wondering if little kids could get hemorrhoids. "We have medicine that makes it feel better."

"No. It just hurts," he replied.

I grabbed his shoulder to turn him around. He moved as though he was half frozen.

Really weird, I thought again.

Reaching up to grab the tops of his footie-jammies so I could pull them down to look, I noticed him wince.

He really is sore, I thought, admonishing myself a little for my impatience, remembering from previous encounters that Brendan never shows pain.

The pajamas fell down around his feet, leaving his bare buttocks staring at me...except they didn't look like butt cheeks anymore, they looked more like melted burgers, all bubbly and red.

I gasped.

"Brendan! What happened?" I tried not to scream the words at him, reminding myself how raised voices could shut him down to a place where he was unreachable.

"It hurts," he said.

"I'll bet...what happened?"

"I was cold," he replied. "I tried to warm up by the wood-stove."

"And you bumped into it?" I felt so bad for not watching him more closely, although I knew he was well aware he shouldn't get too close to the stove because it was hot.

"I wanted to get hot like your coffee cup," he said. "I was cold. I like to grab your coffee cup when it's hot to warm up my hands."

"Oh, Brendan." Now I felt ashamed that I hadn't remembered his tendency to take all words literally. Black and white. Hot and cold. *Damn.*

I hugged him quickly around the neck, amazed he wasn't crying. Either of my daughters would have been screaming for medical care by now, but Brendan had just hidden behind his door.

I picked him up, careful not to touch his behind as I took him out to lay him down on the couch...sunny side up.

Later, his little butt cheeks glowed through the zinc oxide I'd coated them with. He slept there for nearly a week, with the rest of the family empathetically cringing at the full moon shining from the sofa.

This story really illustrates two of the characteristics often displayed in Asperger's. The first is their diminished ability to evaluate and relay their level of physical pain. Brendan not only had difficulty describing what he was feeling, which is typical for AS, but seemed to have a limited response to pain as well. For example, one day he broke his arm playing on the slide with other children at school. The school secretary called me to pick him up and take him to the hospital for treatment. When I arrived, I found him sitting in the office. He gave a little glare at the secretary before he turned to look at me. "I told her not to bother you at work Mom, my arm moves just fine." He wiggled his hand at the end of his forearm, which no longer went in a straight line from his elbow to his wrist. The woman behind the desk rolled her eyes and turned back to her work.

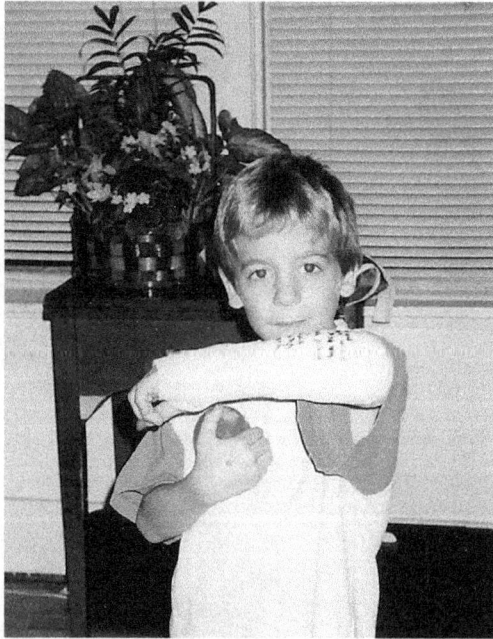

Unfortunately, the story doesn't quite end there, as the following year I received the same call yet again. Both times Brendan had broken his arm on the exact same enclosed slide, trying to climb up from the bottom while other children were sliding down. The first time he explained it was because he was hoping to be shot out on the bottom like a cannonball.

Another lesson we both learned that first day was not to expect even doctors to understand Brendan's differences unless they were already familiar with him. As the doctor went to set his arm, he asked Brendan whether he would like a numbing shot for the pain, before pulling the broken bones back into place. As Brendan was terrified of needles, he naturally declined. Before I could intervene, the doctor had done the deed. Brendan's eyes rolled back into the back of his head, his legs began bicycling through the air, and he went into a series of convulsions. His brain was simply unable to cope with the added stimuli. Had I taken the moment first to explain Brendan's difficulty with understanding outcome, I think the situation would have resulted in a less painful experience for all of us.

However, the next year, when the other arm was broken – he gladly chose to have the shot.

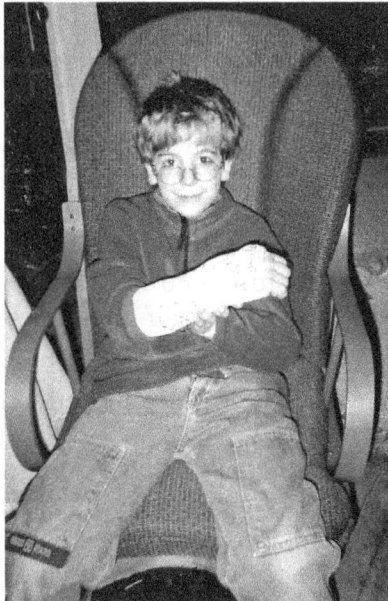

His pediatrician once informed me, research had suggested perhaps the nervous system structure in people with AS was affected by the difference in their brain's response to outside stimuli.

It became apparent Brendan did not feel pain until his tolerance point was reached, which appeared to be much higher than most. After a couple of incidents like these in Brendan's early childhood, I made a point to notify the school administrators, and his teachers each year, that if he mentioned any sort of pain at all, they were to call me immediately. Eventually, I made certain it was written into his IEP each year, which helped to make certain all the people who interacted with him were informed.

If your child is experiencing any difficulties in school, make certain all of their teachers and counselors are informed of their AS diagnosis. An Individualized Education Plan, commonly referred to as an IEP, should be designed for every AS student. This will not only allow for special accommodations to help them work in an NT setting, but also helps to head off potential issues by opening communication lines between schools, counselors and parents.

I also found this step needs to be repeated with each new teacher. In our school system, records were not forwarded to the next grade's teacher, in order to protect students from being categorized by previous data.

The other AS response demonstrated here is their tendency to attempt to hide from conversations they don't know how to begin. Unsure how to ask for help, they will often try to avoid troublesome situations entirely. Rather than ask for help or advice, it is common for them to try to hide rather than face the problem, even when the situation itself does not seem at all difficult to deal with from an NT perspective.

In 2009, the New York Times reported a 13-year old boy with Asperger's living on the subway in New York for 11 days, riding from train to train in order to avoid going home. The boy had not completed an assignment in school, and after being scolded there, had called his mother, who had already heard of the situation, and told him they were going to have a talk.

In the case of Brendan, he had simply chosen to hide behind his door, rather than tell anyone he was injured, although
the burns had to have been excruciating, even for an individual
with a high pain tolerance.

Because of this unwillingness to ask for help or confront
the source of discomfort, you may need to outline for the AS child
the steps they should take to evaluate their own pain level, and
provide appropriate recommendations for each level on the scale.

I discovered this early on, as Brendan would stand in a
shower until the water turned absolutely frigid, curling into a
ball under the cold water while his teeth chattered and he shook
like a leaf. Explaining the water heater only was able to heat so
much water at a time, and when the temperature started to drop
he should finish quickly and get out of the shower, seemed to be
an explanation for what should be intuitive. But intuition is not
a strong suit in a child with AS, and defining solutions to potential problems before they arise can help them to cope.

Be certain to engage them frequently, asking them how
they feel, what they have experienced in their day and how they
reacted to situations they encountered. Teaching them the skills
needed to critically examine life's moments is one of the best
things you can do as a parent.

Lesson of this story...explain, explain, explain, at the risk
of annoying them. It pays off in the long run.

Chapter 8

Underwarrior

"Mommmmmm...Brendan's freaking out!"

My daughter came running into the kitchen, her words punctuated by the bobbing heads of her friends who followed along behind her. Remnants of her birthday cake speckled their clothing, leftovers of an earlier food fight. One of the boys was shaking his head and looking rather disgruntled, as though he was an old man griping to his cronies.

I wiped my dishwater hands on the towel next to the sink; wishing parenting was as mundanely easy as keeping a house clean. My mind added"...*or even as easy as the first two*," before I could stop the thought. I sighed and headed past the rolling eyes and clucking of the gaggle of teenagers gathered in the kitchen.

Brendan stood next to the driveway, poised like he was heading off an imaginary attacker. Bent over at the waist in defense mode, he pointed a large stick into the air. According to Brendan, it was a staff. He was bare-chested; his ribcage still showing a gangling awkwardness I knew soon would be gone. He almost looked like a victoriously triumphant pre-pubescent male showing off for the girls. Almost.

If it wasn't for the pair of white cotton briefs he had stretched out over his head, and the white socks on his hands.

Egads! I tried to think fast. *How do you explain what isn't wrong, but is?*

My planning time was cut short as he spun around with the staff and saw me standing there on the porch.

"Hi, Mom."

His voice still squeaked like a young boy's. As is typical with Asperger's kids, he didn't seem fazed at all by the other kid's responses to him. I suspected he might not have noticed.

"Hi Bren. What's up?" I asked.

"I'm Underwarrior. I'm a Suuuuuperhero," he answered.

"I see that. What are you battling?"

"Bugs."

"Are you winning?" I was mentally still working on how I was going to handle the underwear thing, or if I should just let it go.

"The more I fight them, the more of them show up," he replied. "I had to put a facemask on 'cause they were flying in my ears," he added. His eyes peered through the leg holes at me, making his face look somewhat distorted. "I couldn't find my ski mask."

"Maybe I should help you find your ski mask so the bugs have a harder time getting in your eyes. You would look more like a real superhero then, too."

"OK."

We walked towards the house together, and the back door opened, spitting out the stream of birthday teenagers. One of them sneered, "Look... its poopy pants!"

Brendan took a swing with the staff.

I turned back to Brendan and motioned for him to set the stick on the porch before we went in to begin our search for the missing ski mask. We went inside and closed the door, leaving his opponents outside.

"Bren?"

"Yeah?"

"It kind of grosses some people out you would put underwear on your face because of where they usually are..." I started the sentence, but I knew it probably sounded a little corny from a logical perspective. Brendan was always logical.

"They're clean." he countered.

"I'm sure they are, but some people are still going to think it's weird. They won't understand," I added.

"Yep."

I located the facemask buried under last winter's mittens and pulled it out. "Here you go."

"Thanks, Mom."

"You're welcome. That should keep the bugs out of your eyes and your ears."

"Facemask Man isn't as cool though," he pointed out.

"Bugs won't care." I said.

"True," he agreed as he headed for the door.

"Want a flyswatter?" I called after him.

"Nah. Staff's bigger." he replied.

I nodded, then turned and walked back to the house, knowing he would grow from the battle ahead.

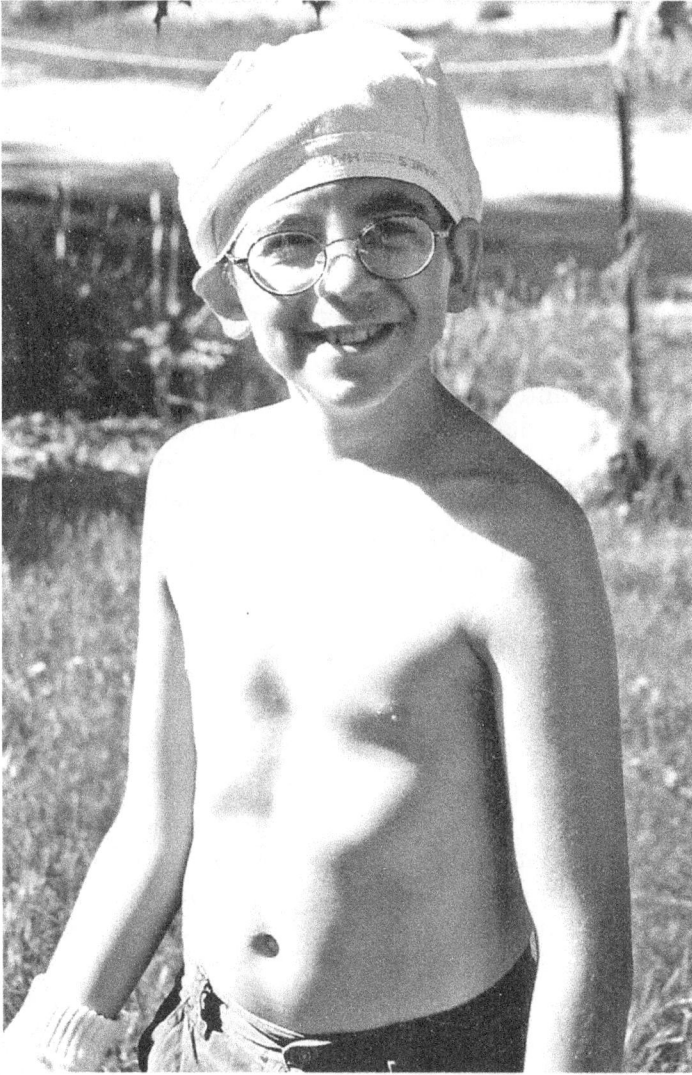

Being a Mom to a child with Asperger's has its challenges, not the least of which is trying to get other kids to tolerate them, and their unusual behavior.

Public school is where many of these kids find themselves, as the typical nuclear family unit has generally progressed to being composed of two wage-earning parents in an economy that seldom allows one parent to stay home with the children. Even if one parent is able to stay at home and school the child, homeschooling tends to set these kids even further behind in supplementing their deficient social skills. Needing more, not less socialization to ready them for adulthood typically means homeschooling has less to offer in this area, regardless of whether it might seem an easier "fit" during childhood. Unless parents can afford to send their children to private schools that specialize in Asperger's, these kids have a tough road on the path to socialization. Yet today's economy often leaves little choice for most families.

The public school system in the U.S. is filled with students from middle class suburbs; all modeling behaviors, mannerisms, clothing and even pursuits to fit in with the other students in their social classes. Being like everyone else has become the rule and not the exception, with the occasional unique student being peer-pressured until they become more like the majority. In today's society, fitting in is all-important for kids. This is true from wearing designer clothes, to gathering together in cliques. The "in" club is no longer the debate team or the science club, but more likely a group comprised of video gamers or sports buffs.

Children with AS are unlikely to conform to the conventional. They may try to wear their Halloween costume to school because it received attention at the last Halloween party. They may wish to read their poem aloud in the cafeteria at lunchtime to an unwilling audience, because adults appreciated it the night before at a dinner party. They may show off their juggling skills while waiting for the bus because they were praised during an exercise designed for motor skills. They are starving for a pat on the back due to their daily difficulties in gaining acceptance.

Being an Asperger's student in middle school and high school in these peer-driven environments offers little but derision, from teasing and name-calling to outright aggression. Bullying is a common occurrence in the life of children with Asperger's. Even students who are more accepting of those with differences will often eventually side with the majority, so as not to be banished to the minority they were trying to protect. At this point, public school in the U.S. is often simply a blunt initiation to the "dog eat dog" world that exists in America today.

In time, those who do not quite fit in, often learn to accept that keeping silent about the aggression that goes on against them is considered "honorable". As a parent, if you stop hearing about difficulties with their peers and your child is in a public school, it would behoove a call to their school counselors to have them check up on their daily interactions with other students. In this parent's experience, it often means they have gone underground and have just advanced to the standpoint that telling a grown-up is not "cool". Generally, the difficulties are still there; they are simply learning through daily encounters to find another way of dealing with the problem, yet not necessarily in a manner best suited to benefit them in the long run.

Try to establish a positive open line of communication with the school guidance counselors. If you don't hear from them (and you likely won't), contact them once a month just to let them know you are involved and caring regarding the needs of not only your child, but also their classmates and the relationships between them.

Although typical teens place emphasis on being and looking "cool," teens with Asperger's may find it frustrating and emotionally draining to try to fit in. As well, if they have not developed a grounded sense of character and self-esteem within themselves, they are often naïve and too trusting, which can lead to teasing, bullying and even coercion.

These teens have the desire to make friends, but having learned of their differences, they hold back from interacting with other students. All of these difficulties can cause teens with Asperger's to become withdrawn and socially isolated and to experience depression or anxiety.

Alternatively, those who have managed to find their sense of self-esteem, may begin to view other students as inferior.

Despite their challenges, some teens with Asperger's syndrome are balanced enough to be able to make and keep a few close friends through their school years.

Some of the classic Asperger's traits may also work to their benefit. Since teens with Asperger's are typically uninterested in following social norms, fads, or conventions, the door is left wide open for creative thinking and the pursuit of original interests and goals. In addition, their preference for order and honesty, combined with their often above average intelligence, may lead them to excel in the classroom, and as young citizens.

83

It's part of your balancing act, keeping them above their growing pains, while simultaneously keeping them grounded with the rest of us.

Chapter 9

Raising a Dragon

"I'm a dragon," said the young man. At fifteen, he was sure he knew all about life, though his lengthiest conversations had so far been inner dialogue.

Fire sparked from behind his eyes as he looked at me, daring a debate on the subject.

"I know," I replied.

I'd seen the egg hatch with my own eyes, it being one of my own. It seemed a hundred years ago, back in the cave-like hospital room, a padded nest where the world around could not hear the mewling cries of the newly born dragon.

I caught his glare. His dark eyes briefly flickered a look of triumph.

"Humans might do chores, but dragons don't," he continued.

"Well...until you perfect your fire-breathing technique, you'll need to carry in firewood to keep our cave warm."

I patted myself mentally on the back for my parenting skills, pleased by my little segue.

"Dragons prefer cold caves."

My sigh escaped as years of patience sailed away upon its breath.

"Now."

It was the best I could do.

The burning scowl he shot over the tops of his wire rim glasses looked as though we really might not need firewood much longer. Even the pimple on the end of his nose looked as though it might erupt at any moment, spewing caustic dragon juice at me.

I turned away so he would not see my fear; my worry. *Could I have spawned such a creature? Would he slay us as we lay asleep in our beds, tossing our bones into the depths of his lair once he'd feasted upon our flesh?*

I turned back to face him.

"You're kinda cute when your scales stick up like that. Don't forget the kindling."

Ah...the joys of Asperger's.

I returned to stirring the pot of minestrone on the stove, knowing I was minutes away from a lengthy argument about the need for meat in the carnivore diet.

I mentally prepared.

The phone rang in the other room; he ran to answer it. I summoned patience when his voice animated in response to the caller, knowing the distraction meant we were now going to replay the firewood scene.

"Hey Soulwind," he spoke loudly into the receiver, as though the sound actually needed to travel the five miles to his friend's house.

They each had "dragon" names. Brendan's was Korica Firetail.

Perhaps due to his IEP, he and his teachers had compromised when he'd insisted on using it in school. Assignments would have his "human" name; stories could have his "dragon" name. He'd failed classes for an entire semester in order to earn the right, with all of his work going into an "Unidentified Student" pile.

Life was a little easier now.

I eavesdropped maternally as his voice lowered, intuitively detecting a hushed urgency.

"Did they say yes?"

The reply must have been favorable, as Korica's jaw set in approval and his head nodded up and down.

Most neurotypical kids might blurt out a passing phrase such as …"Sweet"…"Awesome"… or "Cool."

But dragons speak more using unconscious body language.

I was experienced in dragon-speak. I could tell he was excited by how rapidly his head bobbed.

He wandered to his bedroom, closing the door before pushing the speakerphone button on his phone.

I smiled.

Totally unaware of the audience now standing outside his door, he went on...

"I'm going to ask my Mom for martial arts lessons. Then I'll teach you what I learn, too."

I made a mental note to follow through with tai-chi classes, not yet ready to arm the creature.

"What kind of weapons will you use?"

Safety Mom alert went off like an FBI wiretap alarm.

I held my breath, straining to hear the tinny speaker-phone reply.

"Mostly swords," came the clipped answer.

Who would have dreamed there could be more kids as strange as mine living this close to us? A fleeting thought of some sort of toxic radiation in the area zapping all human eggs in utero came to mind.

"Rivermoon's going to study bombs; then we'll have it all." Korica's monotone voice echoed in my head.

I stood there, torn between the desire to run for the yellow pages where I might find help...(was it a psychologist or psychiatrist?)...and the instinct to hear the rest.

"2012 isn't that far away."

Good...I had time.

I became aware of the soup bubbling in the kitchen, but decided this cauldron needed my attention more.

"I talked online with the White Dragon." Korica's voice was low again.

"Oh wow." The speakerphone reply was flat, lacking the usual enthusiasm expected from the words.

"She says she's already transforming, and we will all finish our transformations into our dragon bodies before the Mayan calendar ends."

The Mayan calendar?

"She says there will be a giant battle before the end of the world as prophesied by the calendar, and the outcome will be up to us." The repeated words poured out of his mouth hurriedly, quite unlike the succinct dragon-speak to which I was accustomed.

"Only if we are truly prepared can we save the world." His voice grew loud and commanding in his passion.

"While the humans are busy destroying the earth, we must prepare and learn, so when the time comes, and we are

88

transformed into our physical dragon selves, we will be ready to survive the aftermath. We will need to be ready to rebuild what remains."

I walked back to the kitchen and opened the refrigerator, looking for last night's leftover chicken to add to the soup.

My son believes he is a reincarnated dragon. At this point, I would have to say this isn't merely a blip in the chapters of his childhood, but rather his own personal defining and obsessive interest. One of the most prominent characteristics of Asperger's kids is that each of them has a subject in which they are avidly interested, often to the point of obsession. Some choose a very mechanical subject; some are very scientific. With Brendan, it ended up being a focusing on the actual differences between he and the rest of us Neurotypicals.

The tendency for high intelligence and the inclination to become very interested in, even preoccupied, with a particular subject, can be your child's best asset. Often this preoccupation can lead to a specific career at which the adult with Asperger's can be very successful.

In my experience, each child goes through a number of phases of these enveloping interests. They tend to be things where data can be memorized and absorbed, giving the child something they excel in.

Some of our current cultural trends actually help to develop these tendencies, as the Pokemon® card phase demonstrates. When Brendan was young, he knew (and likely still does) all of the details for each card. He could recite off, without looking, what power level each had in each arena, and statistical data for each character.

Later his interest evolved into dragons, as he began to notice other parts of his personality, and identified with this under-appreciated and extinct species, from a very personal perspective. From that point, his evolvement went on to envelop reincarnation, evolution, and alternative planes of existence.

Some AS individuals are involved in very concrete and engineering type subjects like trains, patterns, and solar systems. Others are more involved with the abstract such as art, music, or intangibles.

Some children with Asperger's and even with classical autism are savant in particular skills, such as music, mathematics, or languages. Mozart is a great example.

Before kindergarten, Brendan was interested in most of the things described above to some extent. Admittedly he seemed a little advanced for his age. At age 3 he designed his first elevator out of an oatmeal box, complete with pulley systems to bring matchbox cars up to the next level of a structure. He mapped the correct positioning of the planets in the sky with stickers of the solar system on his ceiling at the age of 4. Nothing seemed to really stand out as one nearly obsessive interest, until the Pokemon® cards.

Because the Pokemon® trend happened before the subject of Asperger's became a national discussion, his memorization of Pokemon® character details went fairly unnoticed. Pokemon® cards were all the rage during his elementary school years. Most of the kids had them, traded them, and literally obsessed over finishing their collections. So when Brendan began memorizing every little detail on each card, it seemed typical, and for a time helped him fit in with his peers. Eventually, they became uncomfortable listening to him recite data facts, and began avoiding him once more. They just wanted to trade.

Asperger's kids are known for carrying on one-sided monologues about their subject of choice, which can be nearly intolerable for their audience. Having a limited sense of understanding for other's body language and social hints, they will often describe their interest in too much detail. They'll continue in depth about the subject, unaware of their listener's discomfort, until the listener attempts to reroute the conversation. If you know someone with Asperger's, I'm sure you've been that audience.

When Brendan finally transitioned from memorizing and mentally categorizing all of the Pokemon® characters, when he was about 9, to researching the characteristics of historical interpretations of dragons, I assumed it was simply another phase. It seemed perfectly logical to me for a child with his intelligence, rote memory skills and creative process, to use his talents to investigate any subject in such depth.

Fantasy, which is definitively where I would have placed dragons in the scheme of things, seemed a perfect choice as well, for someone who needed to escape the day to day taunting from his peers. I encouraged him to write fantasy stories with his dragon characters, as he is a very good writer. I even had hopes it could someday be a skill that would help support his future. Perhaps offering him independence in a manner where he would find life comfortable.

Little did I know he would actually come to a point where he totally invested in his own research, believing with absolute certainty dragons not only existed, but that he and many of his friends were reincarnated dragon souls, waiting in human forms to be morphed into their mature dragon selves. Ready, when the earth someday needs them to take over and clean up the mess we humans have made.

Since an obsessive interest is simply a characteristic of Asperger's, I admittedly try not to worry too much about the outcome. Still hoping it will eventually adapt into a more workable version that can fit not only Brendan's needs, but offer him a more settled place in society as an adult.

Currently, he is realizing he has great success in Institutional Technology, and is exploring ways he can use the field to support both his personal endeavors and career goals.

Of course, he is now 18, so I'm also keeping an eye on his back for the wings he was certain were growing there, just in case I'm the one who is mistaken.

Following is one of the poems Brendan wrote when he was about 13, a time when he wrote nearly constantly to express his feelings. I found this one in the rubbish, alongside about 100 others he had discarded.

Go Ahead and Stare

Surrounded by men,
Chased from my den,
Chaos has reigned,
My heart has been pained.

These beasts can't accept
Their minds are inept.
I'm different from them,
And so they condemn.

Go ahead and stare,
It's not like I care.
My wings are unfurled,
It's the end of the world.

(Brendan Townsend 2007 - Age 15)

Chapter 10

The Exorcism

The summer before Brendan's 16th birthday his father and stepmother took him to an exorcist

His father referred to them as "demon chasers".

Brendan, who had asked to spend the summer at his father's house, seemed to find the whole thing rather humorous, and simply stated, "...it didn't seem to do much of anything."

I wasn't surprised.

Nor was I surprised his father believed "the problem" might be as simple as being possessed by demons.

According to Brendan, it took two of the demon chasers to try and heal him. According to his father, they were renowned experts with numerous coups. I pictured my son's soul hanging from their scalp belts.

The situation had arisen when his stepmother found a borrowed book of Wicca hiding under the car seat on the way home from church. They promptly stopped at the nearest garbage can, determined to dispose of the evil-provoking thoughts before their world could be infiltrated.

"I wouldn't take this sort of thing from *my* kids, and I'll not take it from *yours*," snapped his stepmother to me.

I believed her.

Brendan had recently been expressing his disbelief in the Christian religion and its testaments. Advocating knowledge as the best way to learn understanding, I had encouraged him to read about all types of religion so he could form his own beliefs. Although I had not known specifically about the Wicca book, I wasn't surprised it was the choice read of someone whose main interests at the time were dragons and wizards.

More upset about the loss of the book than the attempt to save his soul, Brendan called afterward to say he might like to come home. He said he missed the sunshine; he felt out of place in the city, in a concrete world where all the noise was just the same. He said he missed the birds calling and the wind blowing free.

Safety Mom wanted to get in the car. Another part of me, though, knew this was simply the first of many encounters with conformity he was going to deal with in his lifetime, and coming from the place of love his father was actually trying to offer, was likely one of the safest ways for him to learn how to deal with it.

If it was handled correctly.

I questioned him, "Did it hurt?"

"No," he admitted.

"You knew they were not going to understand why you were reading it, right?" I went on.

"Of course," he said.

"You know Dad loves you?"

"Yep."

"Told you to make sure you didn't take the stuff you've been reading to Dad's," I threw in.

"Yeah, I know."

I love the way he always just accepts the responsibility of his choices. *Some of us could learn from that.*

"Where did you get the book?" I asked him.

"From a teacher," he said.

"Dang." That made it a little harder. "Can we just buy a new one?"

"She had notes in it. She told me it was important to her and to be careful with it."

The fix became bigger, but I knew it was still just the small problem.

"You'll have to buck up, buy a new one, and admit you were foolish to take it to your Dad's." I switched from friend to Mom.

"Yep."

"Remind me when you get home and we'll do it together."
I felt like Brendan had stepped forward, and I was proud to be standing beside him.

"OK."

"You know your Dad loves you and that's why he's acting this way. He has to grow too."

"I know."

"Love you, buddy," I said.

"Love you, Mom."

"Talk to you soon."

"Bye."

The phone went silent.

It can be very frustrating as a parent of a child outside the norm, who has come to a point of understanding and acceptance, only to see others treat them inappropriately due to their condition.

This can be especially frustrating when it is other family members, or people close to your child. Most days, it seems there's barely enough time to deal with being an Asperger's parent. The realization of the need for advocacy in order to protect your child from the potential of damaging statements and actions of others, and in some cases even the education of those persons, can be truly overwhelming.

When my son described to me how his father had reacted to the book he was reading, I was appalled at what I felt to be a lack of concern for how Brendan would absorb his response emotionally. Upon further reflection, and after speaking with Brendan, I realized it was not affecting him as deeply as I feared. Precisely because of his Asperger's, he was emotionally insulated, and far less aggrieved than an NT child might have been. Brendan was merely amused, whereas I was nearly livid with anger at what I viewed as a personal attack against him. Brendan's seemingly mature reaction made me reevaluate my own response before running, sword in hand, to his defense.

Thinking deeply about the situation, I came to some conclusions I found valuable.

I knew his father truly loved him, and although his actions seemed extreme, he truly meant to make life easier for Brendan. Being a devout Christian, his response to something of which he had no control, was to turn it over to a higher power, hoping the power of prayer alone would be sufficient to fix the "problem".

As Brendan and his father are very different in the way they approach finding solutions, I realized I had been unreasonable in assuming his father would understand Brendan's need for more detailed information on religion itself. Asperger's Syndrome does not lend itself well to faith without data.

Brendan had come to me a number of times after being in church with his father, wanting to know how people could believe in something so wholeheartedly when there seemed to be little concrete evidence to back up their manifest, the Bible.

I, uncertain where my own beliefs began and ended as well, suggested he put more research into trying to understand many different religions before dismissing his father's belief system entirely.

It seemed only natural someone currently fascinated with dragons and past lives, should choose to read more about Wicca, which as I understood it, is a religion based significantly on magic.

Looking at it more deeply, it may have seemed magic could be a perfect solution to overcoming the difficulties of trying to fit his square peg self into the round hole slot carved for him in our cookie-cutter society.

Brendan, at the time, was also showing the first signs of enjoying those very differences, as though he was finding fuel to keep him going in his uniqueness. So the Wicca book really didn't come as a great surprise to me, although it certainly was not what I had in mind when I had made my suggestion regarding religious research.

After considering confronting his father head-on, regarding what I felt to be a traumatic event in the life of a child, I decided to speak to Brendan about the incident instead.

My instinct told me if I tried to confront his father about his actions, which were based upon his Christian beliefs, it would simply institute a defense mechanism on his part. I felt the last thing Brendan needed at that point was to have lessons of Christianity force-fed to him in order to substantiate a parental need for action.

So I decided it would be more beneficial to minimize the impact of the exorcism itself.

Brendan and I had a good talk, covering how people become so terrified and threatened by what they are afraid of that they occasionally overreact, and how the aspect of parental love itself can make those reactions even stronger and less rational. We both knew his father simply wanted him to succeed despite his Asperger's, and have a great life. We just didn't believe it was going to be as easy as praying for someone else to cast out some non-existent demon, but we agreed we understood how it could feel comforting to believe that.

For the rest of his life, there are going to be many people who are not going to accept Brendan for who he is, as most people believe each of us could be better if we only changed in some way. I also believe he has a better chance of success if he can learn to try to understand and accept the motives and reactions of the people around him.

As traumatic as the experience could have been for Brendan, I believe we both think it helped him significantly into seeing things from someone else's viewpoint. As this is one of the hardest things for someone with Asperger's Syndrome to do, the lesson ended up being one of the most valuable he could have gained.

1. get two smoke bombs
2. tape them to your hands
3. clap them together
4. then grab a fake rabbit
5. when the smoke clears, show it to your friends.

B.T.

Chapter 11

The Explosive Plan

Just this morning, I received a frantic voicemail from the mother of my son's best friend. By the end of the message she sounded as though she was nearly having a panic attack.

Her argument was my son was acting strange, which in turn was making her son act strange; and her son wouldn't tell her why, but she declares she never wants my son to call hers again.

So this leaves me with being the bad guy when presenting the news to my son, who thinks the world of her son. The first real best friend he's ever had.

Brendan was still at his father's house, having just spent his 6 weeks living there for the summer.

The mother had said Brendan was calling their house "every ½ hour", and she was sure the boys were "...up to something." When the voicemail started, I thought she was asking me to talk with Brendan, requesting he alter his weird behavior in a way that would make her more comfortable.

Her final words though, "You can tell him to stop calling here at any frickin' time of day," made me less confident an adjustment was going to be enough to placate her. Her message finished with a few words for me, "I don't think *you* want to deal with *me* if he involves my son."

I called Brendan.

"What's up?"

"Nothing much," he answered.

"Hmmm... I don't quite believe that. Rivermoon's mom left me a message and she's *very* upset. Seems you've been calling there far too much, like every ½ hour, and Rivermoon won't tell her why. You know I'm trying to help you and not get you into trouble, so I think you'd better talk to me."

I waited.

"Well..." he said. "We had no intention of telling any adults, and Rivermoon's mom can never find out, but you remember how Rivermoon is into explosives...like I mean, really, really into them?"

"Yes." I kept my voice monotone, although my heart tried to race ahead of me.

"Well, we have a plan," he informed me. My fears began take a real shape in front of me; a dragon crunching bones to feather its nest.

"And Rivermoon is your leader?" I asked him.

"No," he assured me. "But he is in on all of it."

"On what?" I kept it simple...a two-word click. *I'm getting pretty good at combination locks.*

"The human race is destroying the world. They're too stupid to even see they are doing it. They think they are the center of the universe, but they are actually the Destructors. He said it with a capital "D".

Now I understood why the boy's mother was upset. Their plan to fight the system had evoked her parental concern, but I found it impossible to be angry at a spurt of idealism. Afraid of my own power to guide it wisely perhaps, but not angry.

"It's the government. It's corrupt," he went on. "They need to be taken down and replaced." He spoke as if he had intimate knowledge, although I knew it was just a baby dragon's impression of something outside of its egg that might stop it from hatching.

"Lots of people in our country would agree with you. You're not alone," I said. "It's why we vote on leaders, and make proposals on issues to be changed," I continued. "Many people have tried to change the system."

"They just do little things that don't make any difference in the big whole," he said. "It's not like us. We are going to make a big difference." "The *Others* weren't prepared," he spoke with a reverence for those who had gone before him. "Of course we won't be bothering to try for a few years, as we are too young to do it anyway," he added. "By then, we will know how to get the necessary equipment. The stupidity has to stop."

I was afraid he could feel my concern, although I tried to hide it.

"But we are a community, Brendan." I argued. "Don't you see, we *are* the group of people who would be hurt. We have to make decisions together that we all agree on or we become simply zealots. I understand why you're upset, and in many respects I agree with you, but if you try to make change that way you are just a terrorist ...a fanatic."

Good, he was grunting a little. It was a tic he had when he was uncomfortable. He seemed off-balance and confused. Exactly what my words had hoped for. I wanted him to think deeper.

"The good guys work as a team to make the bad guys give up, and if you aren't on the team, you are just a crazy person we will try to lock up so you can't hurt us. You have to stay with us or you will look like you're on the bad team. Then we'll fight *you* too."

I breathed in and listened to his vibe. Was he hearing me?

More grunting; he didn't like the idea of being associated with the bad team. Different, yes. Bad, no.

I didn't think it bothered him we might lock him up. He was ready to be the martyr and Superman his way out of the prison.

More power, I thought...power seems to hold authority.

"Besides, the government has bigger weapons than you and your friends can come up with. They have nukes," I said.

"Ah, but the U.S. is weak," he countered. "They wouldn't want to destroy their own country."

"Others have them, too," I said. "Other countries own a good portion of U.S. soil and *they* might not care."

He sounded like he was having trouble finding his feet, so I let him taste the last bite before I went on.

I strained to feel him through the line again. He felt like...Brendan. Still a kid, younger inside than most, even if he was almost grown on the outside.

I decided to spoon in another bite, perhaps throw off his palate with an abrupt flavor change. "And besides, *they* already know what you're up to. *They* have the advantage and are certainly already prepared to stop your efforts."

"Why do you say that?"

"Because they are listening to all your phone and IM conversations if you've been talking about this while you guys are on the phone and the computer."

I could almost hear him chewing he was grunting so hard.

"I thought so!" he exclaimed. After a moment he went on, "I keep hearing clicking noises on the line, like someone in the other room is picking up the phone, but I know Dad's not home 'cause he's at work."

"Yep, that's probably them." I said.

"Well, they must know we are just kids. We're not ready yet."

If he didn't have Asperger's, I think his voice would have quavered.

"They've had the technology for years." I was merciless. "There are secret agencies all over the world that monitor conversations for key words that signal trouble in the world. Our CIA is just one of them."

"Yeah, it's run by the government," he agreed.

I felt like he was now back on the right side.

"Nope, the CIA doesn't even have to answer to the government. They are totally separate, its part of the rules."

I was beginning to feel more confident about winning in the battle against the non-human child.

"Really?"

I took a breath.

"The CIA can do anything, they don't tell anybody."

I could tell he wanted validation; it's who he is.

"I've known two former CIA officers, one of which was my professor in Science. Both of them said the CIA picks up the best of the best in colleges, kids who have high IQ's, kids who think outside the box and know their stuff." I threw in the double whammy "...kids who show great promise for being trustworthy. They won't take kids who have acted fanatically or gone off on a rampage."

I felt like I'd found the magic key to his video game.

"You can't mess up now, or they will never come and talk to you."

There was a long silence.

"Brendan?" I knew he was there, waiting to be led to safety.

"Really?" he said again.

"Really."

The tone of my voice said, *"I love you, I believe in you, I want you to believe in me."*

Now he needed a goal; a purpose.

"Keep learning the skills you're learning; learn about technology, learn about what the earth needs, learn about methods for change. You may be just the kind of person who can help. We both know you can think outside the box."

"OK."

"Love you, buddy," I said.

"I love you, too, Mom," was his reply.

"Don't call Rivermoon anymore," I said. "His Mom is really mad."

"I know," he admitted. "She changed the answering machine message just for me. It says not to bother calling, because they wouldn't want to talk to me anyway." I could hear his frown.

I thought a moment, reminding myself again he wasn't your average kid. He didn't need me to tell him his feelings didn't need to be hurt.

"Lesson learned," I said. "Maybe you will have to wait until you are adults to figure it out."

"Yep," he said.

"See you Sunday," I reminded him.

"See you Sunday."

It took a conscious thought to flip the cell phone closed.

Hopefully *they* were listening.

If someone is told often enough they are abnormal, don't fit in, and don't measure up, eventually their self-esteem will either crush under the weight of the words, or they will work to find an identity worth believing in.

Unfortunately, many Asperger's teenagers have not survived the difficult years of adolescence, where tolerance for differences in school, home and community are often very limited. Thoughts of suicide are a dangerous commonplace in AS teens, many feeling their differences to be insurmountable, and choosing to end their lives during this challenging period. Amidst hormonal changes, stress with peers, and low self-esteem issues, the teenage years make it tougher to remain calm in the face of life's challenges.

It should come as no great surprise then, in order to be able to look at themselves and find self-worth, these teens often must look further than just what they see in the mirror.

Valuable skills for them can often include music, art or writing, as these areas offer limited framework and great opportunities for creativity. If the AS child can be directed to see self-worth in these creative endeavors and specialties, it can help with the development of a foundation of self-acceptance.

Unfortunately, in the public school system, these areas are being slimmed back due to budget cuts in the arts. The AS child often suffers under the weight of structured academia, finding it offers little in the way of understanding and flexibility. Though the coursework may be easy for them, teaching styles are generally not.

In the case of the teens with AS I have personally known through my son, I saw a trend of anger towards the public school system and government. The teens are bright enough they recognize the stifling air of the environment and wish to change it, but by their very nature feel separate from community. This can lead to extreme behavior in the teenage years, and should definitely be monitored.

High school was a very difficult time for Brendan, as students learned to group together into cliques, often attacking the stragglers who did not fit. A few of these stragglers ended up banding together, primarily due to their shared understanding of being picked upon. It was interesting to me that the first "group" Brendan ever truly joined was a combined force against the clique of students who were picking on them. In Brendan's freshman year in high school, I was called to the school when he had defended another straggler, who was being pushed around by a group of peers, with a staff he had taken into school. Much like his battle with bugs in an earlier chapter, he was determined to prevail against his opponents.

Counseling during formative years can be very helpful, and in most cases necessary. Think of it as an Asperger's training assistant, and be certain to choose a counselor who is familiar with Asperger's Syndrome. (Repeat of the last sentence, as it is so very important.)

Counselors are available at school also, but often are not skilled in handling the needs of AS.

As an added note, in my experience, public school is not necessarily the best place for a child with Asperger's. Alternatively, home-schooling offers little chance for social skills acquisition, and is not generally thought to be a suitable option either. Schools which lean towards a learning through an understanding

113

environment, such as Montessori or Waldorf type schools, or better yet, those designed towards the needs of Asperger's itself, may offer the best fit for most youngsters with Asperger's, but as Brendan never attended one, it is merely supposition on my part.

I can attest that small schools, or those who have a very similar population, are not as beneficial to these students as a school with a greater sense of diversification. Brendan declares, though, that it is the experience of having struggled his way through these environments, which has helped him to develop the strength to withstand the expectations of people and society surrounding him.

Asperger's teenagers are in my opinion no more difficult to rear than NT children (my other two children are NT). The difference, however, is being able to see your children as individuals, without comparison to NT siblings. They are each unique, so you have to keep your eyes open. Even when you think you know what you're doing, you probably need to look again.

Chapter 12

The Storm

It was a late July storm; thunder crashing out of the darkness. A solitary window glowed tungsten at the neighbor's house against the night sky. Every few seconds the trees flashed their shadows on the meadow as lightning bolts dove towards the horizon. The town's fire trucks had all gone by in silent red parade so as not to wake the sleeping residents. Just seconds before, the emergency scanner had reported the Gillespie's down the road had "...numerous fires burning" from a lightning strike. The back door slammed as my mate left the house to join the other volunteer firefighters all jumping in their vehicles to follow the call. "It's ten bucks!" he said jokingly with a gapped-toothed grin as he ran out the back door.

Minutes later the door slammed again. Rising out of bed to see what he may have forgotten, I saw a silhouette backlit by the lightning flashes through the panes of the beveled glass porch door. Slipping on my robe and walking towards the doorway I realized the short figure standing there could not be my partner. Subconsciously I knew it could only be Brendan, standing so still in the pouring rain. I swung open the door. His shape didn't move against the flash of the lightning.

"Bren?"

His head was thrown back, the driving rain pelting his cheeks. Water dripped from the nose-piece of the ski goggles he was wearing. His chin lowered, and his eyes dropped down to look at me.

"Come in out of the storm." Instinctively, I mothered him.

"I want to feel the rain," he replied, not so much in protest as a statement of fact.

My memory skipped time, landing in a puddle where my small bare feet jumped in defiance of my mother's voice. *Safety Mom* reached out to push the enchanting little girl back into the past.

"Then you will have to wait until the lightning passes."

A large droplet fell from his nose to his pouty lower lip.

"But I'm not afraid. I like the lightning,"

"It's not safe." Blunt and terse, I hoped my tone said I would not bargain further.

He looked at me for a long moment, finally pushing the goggles up onto his hairline. Raindrops began to gather on his eyelashes, but he didn't blink. One foot moved in the direction of the house.

"Can I read by candlelight, like they used to in the olden days?"

"Sure...if you promise not to lay down. You might fall asleep. We wouldn't want the house to catch afire."

I didn't want to say yes, his lack of good judgment still worried me, but I held out the peace offering anyway.

"The goggles were a smart idea though," I added.

"That way my eyeballs didn't fill up with rain and make things blurry," he explained.

"Yes, that's what I guessed."

"I can still see the little pieces of lightning that stuck on my eyeballs," he threw in.

"That will go away when you get in the candlelight," I assured him.

"Its OK with me if they stay there. I like lightning."

"Yes, I know. Me too."

He headed up the stairs towards his room, and I closed the door behind him.

One of the traits of AS is a heightened awareness of physical sensations. This may contribute to their fascination with things that appease their need for sensory input, which they often find pleasurable. Some sounds, smells, tastes, and touches are comforting to those with Asperger's, and others will quickly drive them into a state of frustrated anxiety.

Particular fabrics may be distracting and even unbearable against the skin of autistic children. Toddlers will often remove clothing that irritates them, paying no attention to the appropriateness of the situation. Clothing may need to be chosen with these preferences in mind, taking into consideration that if it doesn't "feel" good, it will never get the chance to "look" good. Have your child try things on before you purchase them, so the garment is "child-tested".

Lianne Holliday Willey, a woman who realized she had Asperger's after she reached adulthood, has written about this limitation, stating she could not tolerate the feeling of particular fabrics or clothing that inhibited her, saying she would just remove the items which bothered her the most. (Willey, 1999)

Brendan displayed a remarked aversion to certain fabrics; he could not stand anything close to his skin that was silky or cold, preferring primarily fuzzy soft fabrics, especially cotton or fleece. He basically lived in sweatpants.

Sleeping accommodations may also be affected by these preferences. Some children like the weight of heavy blankets, or the security of "mummy" sleeping bags. Temple Grandin designed a mechanism based on a cattle inoculation gate, which applied pressure to her body and may have helped compensate for her discomfort with physical touch. She found pressure was emotionally and mentally calming to her, and labeled the device a "squeeze machine". (Grandin 1996). My son had a foam pillow "couch", which we kept for his sister's sleep-overs, that he would pull on top of him in order to have the physical weight for comfort. Opening his door in the morning, I would find him buried under all of the things he could accumulate. I never once, however, found him sleeping between the crisp and clean cotton sheets I would put upon his bed.

Another major sensory obstacle for many of these children is sound. Not only did my son ignore most music, he would cover his ears and get visibly upset when we played it loudly. The first musical experience he enjoyed was the instrumental saxophone music played by the musician Kenny G. I think he found this music more tolerable due to the fact it was only one instrument playing, and not a combined sound such as most bands. Now, he has graduated to liking various artists or instrumental sounds. Many of them are classical, but he still generally chooses simple acoustics such as a piano or a single vocal. Even now though, as he approaches adulthood, most music to him can be likened to nails on a chalkboard. He retreats into his room, plugs earphones into his ears, and hums to himself to escape.

Although he doesn't often listen to music, Brendan loves to play on keyboards and recorders. It seems the simple melodies sooth him, and he will quite often head for his own instruments when he finds life stressful.

Brendan, (and myself) have great difficulty separating combined elements of auditory information into sounds, songs, or lyrics we can process, especially if they occur simultaneously. This is sometimes referred to as auditory processing disorder, and seems to be common to those with Asperger's syndrome, though it occurs frequently in NT individuals as well.

Assigning your child a place where they can find quiet when the input is overwhelming, can truly help with the balance they might need, especially in loud environments.

At one point in his elementary years, we had written into Brendan's IEP that he should have a quiet space where he could retreat, when the auditory level of public school became too much. This seemed to work quite well, and furthermore, helped him to understand also how to monitor his own stress level. He learned to determine when he needed to escape the chaos, in order to bring himself back to calmness.

This can be a very helpful tool during the growth years, and lasting well into the needs of adulthood. A quiet place to escape to, can be essential to success.

Chapter 13

Warming the Egg

I reached over to close the damper on the old cast iron woodstove sitting in the corner of the living room. Attempting to slide the poker back under the stove where it was kept, the end of it ran into something solid in what should have been empty space. I leaned down and peered under the front of the stove, spotting a rock tucked away underneath. After briefly wondering why, I continued into the kitchen where I was working on dinner.

The shape of the rock had struck a familiar chord in my memory, but it wasn't until I was peeling a potato that I remembered where I had seen it before. I'd given it to Brendan last year after one of my rock-hunting forays at the Lake Michigan shoreline.

It had looked so perfectly like a very large egg...an egg big enough to contain a baby dragon.

As Brendan's current all absorbing interest was dragons, I'd thought he might like the rock as a decoration for his room. His room was decorated with everything related to dragons and wizards, including numerous Harry Potter memorabilia, his many hand-carved staffs, and a large assortment of primitive scientific instruments. I'd figured it would fit in perfectly.

"It looks like a dragon egg," I'd said, as I presented him with my "find".

"Sure does," he had replied. "Thanks Mom."

"You're welcome. I thought you'd like it for your room."

I finished a potato and dropped it in the pan of water heating on the stove, forgetting to slice it first. Reaching into the warm water to pull out the potato, I suddenly made the connection...

"Was he warming the *egg?*

A small smile from the thought landed on my lips, as I found once again the simple pleasures in being the mother of a boy who did not break windows with baseballs.

I finished peeling the last potato, sliced it and dropped it in the water with the rest. Walking out of the kitchen, I went to grab my camera, certain I was right...and wanting to capture the smile to take out and reuse another day.

Lying on the floor to take the photo, I had a brief worry the rock might explode from the heat given off by the woodstove. I'd seen that happen once at a campfire, when we had dragged rocks from the river to ring the fire. Eventually I determined it was just as likely the rock would actually hatch, and decided to leave it under the stove to let Brendan finish his experiment.

When he went to bed that evening, the rock was gone.

Rather surprised I had been wrong, and totally embarrassed I was at the point of conjuring up strange stories, I asked him about it at breakfast the next morning.

"I get cold at night, so I put it under the woodstove to heat it up so I could sleep with it," he explained.

I laughed.

"Well, that makes perfect sense, Brendan. People used to have warming pans they put in their beds at night in the old days." Giggling again, I realized the photo was now going to be a simply a reminder of my own silliness.

"I know." It was his usual reply.

"I remembered it was the rock I gave you from the beach, and I thought maybe you were trying to hatch it," I admitted with a smile.

"Well, that, too," he replied as he looked at me with surprise on his face that I'd guessed. "I take it into sleep with me at night so it can bond with me before it hatches."

"Good idea," I said. "Bonding is important."

"Yep," he agreed.

We all understand "fitting in" somewhere is important. Whether we meld with a group of people, are active in the community, or have strong family ties that maintain us, having someplace to call "home" is paramount to our emotional survival. Even Asperger's kids hope to fit in; they just show less inclination towards social connections than the NT child.

Children with Asperger's find it even harder to find a community of people who understand them. Their families and classmates are likely fairly homogenous, often making it difficult for them to relate. Seeing the world differently, they are like foreigners in a strange land.

Prior to the label of Asperger's, it was suggested the word "autism" meant "escape from reality", coined from Eugene Bleuler in 1912. An authority on psychology, he also coined the title of schizophrenia.

The imagination offers a place of acceptance; somewhere where all things can be possible, accepted, and perhaps even embraced.

Tony Attwood noted in his works that imagination was a place very often visited by the older child with Asperger's, especially during their teenage years.

If a world does not exist within their reality, then they will often create an alternative which suits them better.

It can be rather common for these children to fabricate a new world, even if it reaches into the imaginary or supernatural. The difference between the child diagnosed with Asperger's doing this and the NT child, is in the reason why. The child with AS constructs an imaginary environment around their own hopes and desires, having little or nothing to do with influencing others. Their worlds are built to accommodate their own needs.

The NT child, on the other hand, often may build these environments to impress, amuse, or even sidetrack others. Calculation is often a factor.

Being accepted in some capacity is a valid human need. Each of us needs to know we have a purpose, value, or ideal that keeps us going in the path we choose. Without that, we wither and fail to thrive. Whether NT or AS, we need a connection to something larger than ourselves to truly grow.

Another book, written by a man with Asperger's, tells how his interest in fantasy helped him to become a comic strip writer as an adult. He learned to use his skill in a way that offered a living doing something he felt comfortable doing, and was good at. (Robison, 2007)

Brendan loves to write. He created many fantasy stories about dragons during his teen years, that I suspect may grow into something he may publish later.

Besides, if a rock ever does hatch into a formerly dormant dragon, he will be the world's expert we will all look to for advice.

Chapter 14

Hiding in a "Normal" Cloak

This fall, as Brendan headed off to a new school district for his Junior and Senior years in high school, he decided to modify his behavior and appearance in order to fit in by hiding under a "normal cloak".

"Nobody is going to see me as the weird dragon boy," he said. "It's a perfect opportunity for me to make friends without the labels I've always been judged by."

As the days of September closed in, I wondered if perhaps he could really pull it off. He began dressing differently, looking in the mirror to see how his clothes looked. He tried new hairstyles, straightening his long wiry curls into a burnt looking mop one day, then tying it back the next. He trimmed up the beard he had begun growing at age 13 and began to look more like a young man than Oscar the Grouch.

Could it really have been just the label? Doubt began to spring up. *What if I had just been perpetuating a fallacy?*

There was a new spring in his step; I could see he was excited about this new journey.

Looking at him closely, the new Brendan seemed to have grown far beyond his previous limitations.

The first day of school came, and we drove to his new school district, where the programs seemed to better suit his needs. I dropped him off at the bus stop where I watched him get on the bus with the now familiar feeling of first day trepidation.

I went back home and waited. But the phone never rang.

At the end of the day, I sat at the bus stop in my car, waiting for the yellow bus to pull up and spit out its daily load of youthful energy. Ten minutes late, it screeched to a halt with the familiar brake squeal.

Brendan was the first one off the bus, his long black Halloween cloak from last year billowing out behind him as he leapt from the platform.

I was quick to correct myself...*Don't chastise...remember to support him in his first day...*

He climbed into the passenger seat, stuffing his backpack at his feet.

"How was it? Did you have a good day?"

"It was great!" he answered, digging in his backpack for a book to read on the way home.

"What was your favorite part?" I tried to elicit more detail.

"Metals and jewelry," was his simple reply.

This year, for the first time, he had been involved with choosing his classes. This school had a special needs program, with a dedicated counselor who helped the students navigate through their personal challenges within the public school system. It was a good portion of the reason I was willing to make the long commute each day.

"You didn't wear the cloak in school, did you? You remember how it was against the rules at your old school, right?"

"Naw. I left it in my locker and just put it on while I was waiting for the bus after we got out of class. I was normal, just like everybody else."

I smiled at him. "That's great! Glad to hear it!"

He smiled back and then looked down at his book, while we drove home the rest of the way in silence.

This was when I realized our "experts" had only been partially correct in their evaluation of Brendan, stating that he, and others with AS, would likely never be able to conform enough to society to live an independent life. He did have the capability of seeing what needed to be done to make his way, but would always sort out in his mind what was necessary (in his opinion), versus what wasn't. It was true he was probably always going to seem rather strange compared to most. But strange people were everywhere, many navigating simple paths from their small apartments to their office cubicles, and back again.

The idea the future was as simple as black and white dissolved into grays full of possibilities.

He will likely always need a little guidance as his life evolves through new routines, but I now know there is a lot of warm sandy beach to walk on, between the dangerous surf and shoreline rocks. The unwritten chapters that follow behind these are full of variables, and Brendan and I have both found that cloak shopping is more fun, than we ever dreamed it might be.

Epilogue

One of the things I most worried about as the parent of a child diagnosed with Asperger's was, "Will my child be OK?"

If you share that concern, I want to assure you not only will your child be "OK", there is reason to believe they may be even more significant to the future of humanity than we may have ever suspected. I personally believe you should count yourself fortunate to have experienced a connection with an individual as unique, creative, and intelligent as these kids. I initially considered titling this book "The not so sad story about raising a child with Asperger's"; not only because many Asperger's parents have found it be a rewarding journey, but because the experience offers a wealth of understanding and knowledge into the more subconscious psyche of our species, without the limitations that society imprints on our youngsters.

In my own experience with Asperger's as a parent, I have come to the conclusion that "human instinct" and "intuition" appear to be the missing links in my child's ability to process sensory information.

The visual cues given by people who interact with us, have little effect on the child with Asperger's. We react differently to the sensory triggers of sound and smell. Whereas we may automatically adjust our behavior to adapt to situations based on previous experience, these children do not instinctively make the same adjustments.

By following the techniques written by experts to help with social skills, patterning and routine, I have been able to teach many of the things to my child that he did not learn instinctively. As a parent, I know the desire to land our children into a place where they succeed, is paramount in our priorities.

There is also great news in the work being done to help these children navigate their lives, with the result many of them are now considered to have transitioned off the spectrum altogether. With early diagnosis and intervention, they can often develop the skills that allow them to continue to guide themselves without assistance.

A recent study, which was presented at an international autism conference in Chicago, declared there is a good possibility of 10-20% of recently diagnosed children with autism being able to evolve off the spectrum with proper training and counseling.

Moving off the spectrum does not entail losing any of the benefits of the condition. Intelligence and creativity are unaffected. However, social skills can be learned and difficulties surmounted through the proper framework.

Some will "recover", and others will not. This, too, is just a label waiting to be challenged and clarified.

As our society itself continues to develop further into a diverse collaboration of independent thinkers, graduating away from the norms and status quo resulting from the industrial revolution, I see Asperger's as a step towards that individuality.

One parent, in response to an Asperger's expert, commented that Asperger's was perhaps the next state of evolution. There are statements and facts to support this hypothesis. I myself believe there are definite indications Asperger's is not a disability, but rather just a characteristic paving the way for evolvement into our next phase as the human race.

Perhaps as a genetic evolution, it may allow us the opportunity to recognize what we each are best at, specializing in our own areas of expertise, while offering greater benefits to the entire population. Even better, perhaps someday we will be able to accept our differences, and become a community sharing our combined knowledge of all things, allowing us a better chance at success in a changing world.

Truly, I now believe there is little limitation as to where these children can grow, no plane of understanding they are incapable of reaching, no idea they are unable to comprehend, with the proper teachers. They are intelligent and genuine, and ripe for a future that offers them something in which they can believe. Born without the instincts of human nature which pressure us into conformity, I believe they are poised to help us transition into the evolved stewards of diversity we were meant to become on earth.

During my shared time with Brendan, I have richly grown in ways I never expected as a parent, and as an individual. As you read through these stories, I hope you gain insights which result in your own journey being as rewarding and fun.

As a parent of a child with Asperger's, I congratulate you on your good fortune. Have fun, smile, and know inside, you have helped to create a fellow being who is devoted to taking us into the future using their intelligence, their creativity, and integrity, without boxes.

Here's to the metaphorical dragon being hatched from the egg, incubated by the love offered by the young man who stands watch by its side. We should all value as much the possibility of a better and more thoughtful future.

Thank you, Brendan, for being such an inspirational, valued, and Real Person in the life I was given.

This book is for you.

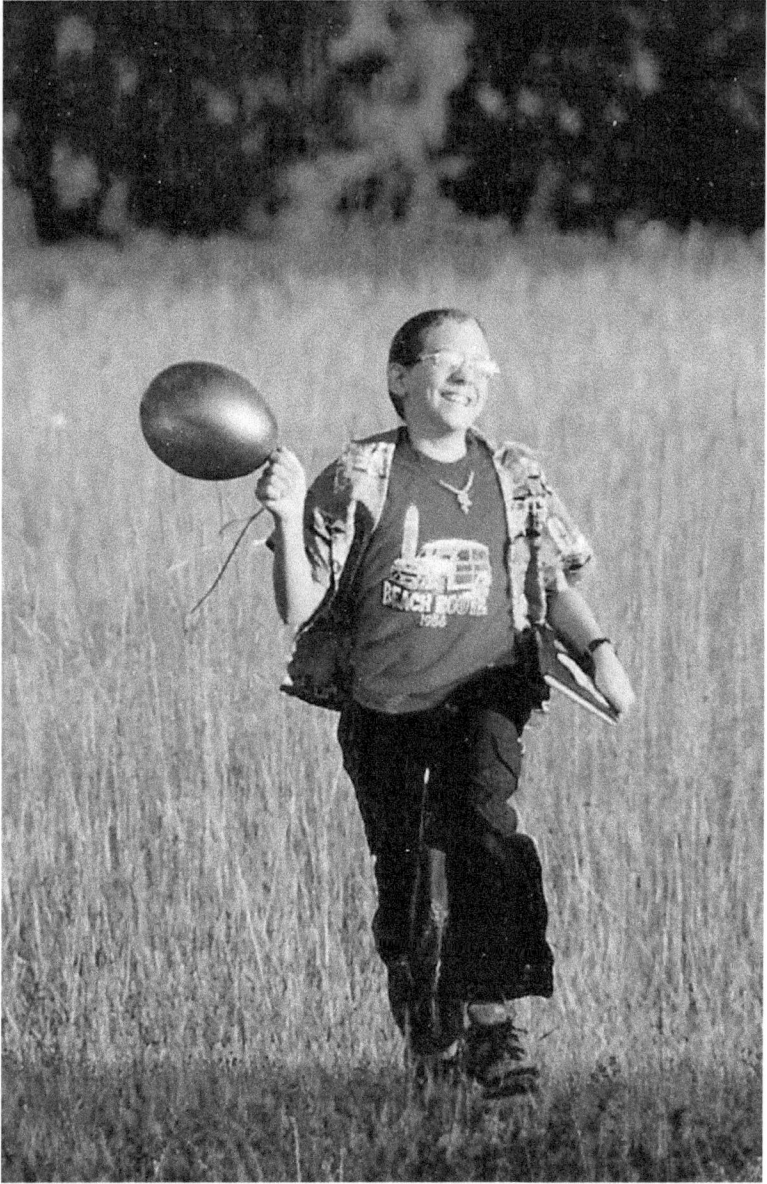

Appendix I

Diagnostic Criteria For Asperger's Disorder 299.80

(Added to DSM IV in 1994)

A. Qualitative impairment in social interaction, as manifested by at least two of the following:

(1) marked impairments in the use of multiple nonverbal behaviors such as eye-to-eye gaze, facial expression, body postures, and gestures to regulate social interaction

(2) failure to develop peer relationships appropriate to developmental level

(3) a lack of spontaneous seeking to share enjoyment, interests, or achievements with other people (e.g. by a lack of showing, bringing, or pointing out objects of interest to other people)

(4) lack of social or emotional reciprocity

B. Restricted repetitive and stereotyped patterns of behavior, interests, and activities, as manifested by at least one of the following:

(1) encompassing preoccupation with one or more stereotyped and restricted patterns of interest that is abnormal either in intensity or focus

(2) apparently inflexible adherence to specific, nonfunctional routines or rituals

(3) stereotyped and repetitive motor mannerisms (e.g., hand or finger flapping or twisting, or complex whole-body movements)

(4) persistent preoccupation with parts of objects

C. The disturbance causes clinically significant impairment in social, occupational, or other important areas of functioning

D. There is no clinically significant general delay in language (e.g., single words used by age 2 years, communicative phrases used by age 3 years)

E. There is no clinically significant delay in cognitive development or in the development of age-appropriate self-help skills, adaptive behavior (other than social interaction), and curiosity about the environment in childhood

F. Criteria are not met for another specific Pervasive Developmental Disorder or Schizophrenia

Bibliography

(1) Asperger, Hans (1944) "Die "Autistischen Psychopathen" [Autistic psychopats in childhood]"

(2) Wing, Lorna (1981) "Asperger's Syndrome, A Clinical Account" http://www.udel.edu/bkirby/asperger/ (3/6/05)

(3) Gilbertson, Ashley (11/24/09) "Runaway Spent 11 Days in the Subways"
http://www.nytimes.com/2009/11/24/nyregion/24runaway.html

(4) Grandin, Temple (1988) "Teaching tips from a recovered autistic." Focus on Autistic Behavior 3.

(5) Grandin, Temple, PhD. (1996) "Thinking in Pictures."

(6) Gillberg, Christopher; copied from "Asperger's Syndrome" by Stephen Bauer, M.D. M.P.H. 03/06/05, http://www.udel.edu/bkirby/asperger/

(7) Attwood, Tony (1998) "Asperger's Syndrome, A Guide for Parents and Professionals" Jessica Kingsley Publishers

(8) Freisleben-Cook, Lois (1995) "A More Down-to-Earth Description" https://groups.google.com/group/bit.listserv.autism/

(9)Lasalle, Barbara (2003) "Finding Ben" McGraw-Hill Publishers

(10) Attwood, Tony (2007) "The Complete Guide to Asperger's Syndrome" Jessica Kingsley Publishers

(11) Holliday Willey, Liane (1999) "Pretending to be Normal" Jessica Kingsley Publishers

(12) Encarta, (8/3/2009) "Definition of Genius"

(13) Kathleen Doheny, WebMD (5/11/2009)
"Study Shows Some Children May 'Move off' the Autism Spectrum"

(14) Townsend, Brendan, "Various notes, poems and thoughts of Brendan Townsend"

(16) Bettelheim, Bruno (1967)
www.autism-resources.com/autismfaq-hist.html   (1/28/10)

(17) Robison, John Elder (2007) "Look Me In the Eye"

Great Online Resources about Asperger's:

www.aspergersyndrome.org

www.nimh.nih.gov/health/topics/autism-spectrum-disorders-pervasive-developmental-disorders/index.shtml

www.cdc.gov/ncbddd/autism/index.html

www.wrongplanet.net/

www.autismtoday.com

www.aspergers.com

www.parentingaspergerscommunity.com

www.autismspeaks.org/what-autism/asperger-syndrome

www.autism-society.org/about-autism/aspergers-syndrome/

www.aspergersnet.org

www.autismdigest.com

www.autism-resources.com

www.community-autism-resources.org

About the Author

Debra Townsend lives in northern Michigan; a solo warrior Mom of three amazing children, cats, dogs and the occasional goat.

A member of Michigan Writers, her articles and short stories have been featured in publications and creative writing competitions including The Healing Garden Journal, YourPlace, NMC Magazine, and the Interlochen Review.

Debra graduated Phi Theta Kappa from Northwestern MI College with a degree in Liberal Arts, emphasizing in journalism and photography.

She carries a pen, her camera, and a sense of humor with her at all times.

www.ingramcontent.com/pod-product-compliance
Lightning Source LLC
Chambersburg PA
CBHW052107090426
42741CB00009B/1708

9 780985 244200